Also by C. K. Williams

Lies   *(1969)*
I Am the Bitter Name   *(1971)*
With Ignorance   *(1977)*
Sophocles' Women of Trachis
   (with Gregory Dickerson)   *(1978)*
The Lark. The Thrush. The Starling.:
   Poems from Issa   *(1983)*
Tar   *(1983)*
Flesh and Blood   *(1987)*

Poems
1963–1983

Poems

1963–1983

C. K. Williams

Farrar Straus Giroux

New York

Library of Congress Cataloging-in-Publication Data
Williams, C. K. (Charles Kenneth).
[Selections. 1988]
Poems, 1963–1983 / C. K. Williams.—1st ed.
Includes index.
I. Title.
PS3573.I4483A6 1988 811'.54—dc19 88-11025

Contents

I Am the Bitter Name [1971]

The Lark. The Thrush. The Starling.
(Poems from Issa) [1983]

With Ignorance [1977]

Tar [1983]

Author's Note

I have omitted several poems from *Lies* and *I Am the Bitter Name*, and have restored the order of sections of the latter to what they were before what now seems an injudicious last-minute change. All of *With Ignorance* and *Tar* has been included. Although the chapbook of poems from Issa, *The Lark. The Thrush. The Starling.*, was published in 1983, the same year as *Tar*, the group of which they were a selection was actually composed from around 1973 to 1976, so I have placed them here before *With Ignorance*.

C. K. W.

Lies

Before This

we got rid of the big people
finally we took grandpa and put half
on the mack truck and half on
the bottom grandma
we locked in with her watches
mommy and daddy had to be cut apart but they
are in separate icebergs you can't
see them under
the red lid

one place or another they are all gone
and it's hard to remember
cars? furcoats? the office?
now all there are
are roomfuls of children sleeping as far
as you can see little mattresses and
between them socks balled up and
underwear and scuffed shoes
with their mouths open.

but how am I here? I feel
my lips move I count breaths I hear somebody
cry out MOTHER HELP ME somebody's hand
touches me peacefully across boundaries
kiss? hit? die? the blankets
harden with urine the fuzz
thins holes come
HOW AM I HERE? MOTHER
HOW AM I HERE?

Even If I Could

Except for the little girl
making faces behind me, and the rainbow
behind her, and the school and the truck,
the only thing between you
and infinity
is me. Which is why you cover your ears
when I speak and why
you're always oozing around the edges,
clinging, trying
to go by me.

And except for my eyes and the back
of my skull, and then my hair,
the wall, the concrete
and the fire-cloud, except for them
you would see
God. And that's why rage howls in your arms
like a baby and why I can't move—
because of the thunder and the shadows
merging like oil and the smile gleaming
through the petals.

Let me tell you how sick with loneliness
I am. What can I do while the distance
throbs on my back like a hump,
or say, with stars stinging me
through the wheel? You are before me,
behind me things rattle their deaths out
like paper. The angels ride
in their soft saddles:
except for them, I would come closer
and go.

Saint Sex

there are people whose sex
keeps growing even when they're old whose
genitals swell like tumors endlessly
until they are all sex and nothing else nothing
that moves or thinks nothing
but great inward and outward handfuls of gristle

think of them men
who ooze their penises out like snail
feet whose testicles clang in their scrotums women
are like anvils to them the world an
anvil they want to take whole buildings
in their arms they want
to come in the windows to run antennas
through their ducts like ramrods and women
these poor women who dream and dream of
the flower they can't sniff it sends buds
into their brain they feel their neural
river clot with moist fingers the ganglia
hardening like ant eggs the ends
burning off

pity them these people there are no wars
for them there is no news no
summer no reason they are so humble they want
nothing they have no hands or faces
pity them at night whispering I love
you to themselves and during the day how they
walk along smiling and suffering pity
them love them they are
angels

The Long Naked Walk of the Dead

FOR ARTHUR ATKINS

As long as they trample the sad smiles of guitars
the world won't burn. The mother speaks to her daughter
and explains: it is the breath of money in the trees
that drives angels; it is the stillness from morning
to morning when the horses of life have fallen
under their traces in the street and shudder and vanish.

It is the man who meets no one who will touch us
with sharp hands that shake over the concrete
like branches. Or the songs muttering on the paths
crisscrossing the grasses. A bench leaning back.
The sweet arms of gardeners. An enemy passing
with sons and grandsons, all just soldiers.

In flesh that only moves and speaks, the players
slide out like empty trailers to the temple country.
Six hundred thousand on the mountain when it opened.
Every word of the scream, six hundred thousand faces.
The dark metal man gleaming in the talons of silence.
Halfway down in the house of suffering, it is starting.

In There

Here I am, walking along your eyelid again
toward your tear duct. Here are your eyelashes
like elephant grass and one tear
blocking the way like a boulder.

It probably takes me a long time
to figure it out, chatting with neighbors,
trying penicillin, steam baths, meditation
on the Shekinah and sonnet cycles

and then six more months blasting
with my jackhammer before I get in there
and can wander through your face, meeting you
on the sly, kissing you from this side.

I am your own personal verb now. Here I come,
"dancing," "loving," "making cookies."
I find a telescope
and an old astronomer

to study my own face with,
and then, well, I am dreaming behind your cheekbone
about Bolivia and tangerines and the country
and here I come again, along your eyelid, walking.

Loss

In this day and age Lord
you are like one of those poor farmers
who burns the forests off
and murders his land and then
can't leave and goes sullen and lean
among the rusting yard junk, the scrub
and the famished stock.

Lord I have felt myself raked
into the earth like manure,
harrowed and plowed under,
but I am still enough like you
to stand on the porch
chewing a stalk or drinking
while tall weeds come up dead
and the house dogs, snapping
their chains like moths, howl
and point towards the withering
meadows at nothing.

The Hard Part

Do you remember when we dreamed about the owl
and the skeleton, and the shoe
opened and there was the angel
with his finger in the book, his smile like chocolate?

And remember? Everything that had been crushed
or burned, we changed back.
We turned the heart around
in the beginning, we closed the blossom, we let the drum go.

But you're missing now. Every night I feel us crying
together, but it's late—
the white bear and the lawyer
are locking the house up and where are you?

The wind walking, the rock turning over with worms
stuck to its haunches—
how will I know what loves me now
and what doesn't? How will I forgive you?

The World's Greatest Tricycle-Rider

The world's greatest tricycle-rider
is in my heart, riding like a wildman,
no hands, almost upside down along
the walls and over the high curbs
and stoops, his bell rapid firing,
the sun spinning in his spokes like a flame.

But he is growing older. His feet
overshoot the pedals. His teeth set
too hard against the jolts, and I am afraid
that what I've kept from him is what
tightens his fingers on the rubber grips
and drives him again and again on the same block.

The Sorrow

with huge jowls that wobble with sad o
horribly sad eyes with bristles with
clothes torn tie a rag hands trembling this
burnt man in my arms won't listen he
struggles pulls loose and is going
and I am crying again Poppa Poppa it's me Poppa
but it's not it's not me I am not
someone who with these long years will
so easily retreat I am not someone after
these torments who simply cries so
I am not so unquestionably a son or
even daughter or have I face or voice
bear with me perhaps it was me who
went away perhaps I did dream it and give
birth again it doesn't matter now I stay
in my truck now I am loaded with
fruit with cold bottles with documents
of arrest and execution Father do you
remember me? how I hid and cried to you?
how my lovely genitals were bound up?
I am too small again my voice thins my
small wrists won't hold the weight again
what is forgiven? am I forgiven again?

The Man Who Owns Sleep

The man who owns sleep
is watching the prisoners being beaten
behind the fence.
His eye pressed to the knothole,
he sees the leather curling into smiles
and snapping, he sees the intricate geography
of ruined backs,
the faces propped
open like suitcases
in the sunlight.

Who is this man
who's cornered the market
on sleeping?
He's not quite finished yet.
He bends over with a hand on his knee
to balance him
and from the other side they see
that clear eye in the wall
watching unblinking.
They see it has slept,

prisoners and guards: it drives them
to frenzies. The whips hiccup
and shriek. Those dead already roll over
and rub their retinas into the pebbles.
The man who owns sleep has had it.
He's tired.
Taking an ice-cream cone
from the little wagon
he yawns and licks it.
Walking away, he yawns, licking it.

Dimensions

There is a world somewhere else that is unendurable.
Those who live in it are helpless in the hands of elements,
they are like branches in the deep woods in wind
that whip their leaves off and slice the heart of the night
and sob. They are like boats bleating wearily in fog.

But here, no matter what, we know where we stand.
We know more or less what comes next. We hold out.
Sometimes a dream will shake us like little dogs, a fever
hang on so we're not ourselves or love wring us out,
but we prevail, we certify and make sure, we go on.

There is a world that uses its soldiers and widows
for flour, its orphans for building stone, its legs for pens.
In that place, eyes are softened and harmless like God's
and all blend in the traffic of their tragedy and pass by
like people. And sometimes one of us, losing the way,
will drift over the border and see them there, dying,
laughing, being revived. When we come home, we are half way.
Our screams heal the torn silence. We are the scars.

To Market

suppose I move a factory
in here in my head in my
breast in my left hand I'm moving
dark machines in with gear boxes
and floaters and steel cams
that turn over and start things
I'm moving in fibers through
my left nostril and trucks
under my nipples and the union
has its bathroom where I think
and the stockbroker his desk
where I love

and then if I started turning
out goods and opening
shops with glass counters and rugs
what if I said
to you this is how men live and I
want to would you believe me
and love me I have my little
lunch box and my thermos and
I walk along like one leg
on the way to work swearing
I love you and we have lunch
behind the boiler and I promise
I love you and meanwhile the oil
flowing switches steam wrenches
metal I love
you and things finish get shined
up packed in streamers
mailed and I love you
meanwhile all this while I love
you and I'm being bought pieces
of me at five dollars

and parts at ten cents and
here I am still saying I love
you under the stacks under
the windows with wires the smoke
going up I love
you I love you

What Is and Is Not

I'm a long way from that place,
but I can still hear
the impatient stamp of its hoof
near the fire, and the green clicking
of its voices and its body flowing.

At my window, the usual spirits,
the same silence. A child would see it
as my clothes hanging like killers
on the door, but I don't, and it
doesn't creak in the hallway for me.

It's not death. In your face
I glimpse it. You are reaching
a hand out comfortingly
though it snarls, plunges,
and you know that the baby

won't look up from its game
of beauty. It isn't love or hate
or passion. It doesn't touch us,
dream us, speak, sing or
come closer, yet we consume it.

Hood

Remember me? I was the one
in high school you were always afraid of.
I kept cigarettes in my sleeve, wore
engineer's boots, long hair, my collar
up in back and there were always
girls with me in the hallways.

You were nothing. I had it in for you—
when I peeled rubber at the lights
you cringed like a teacher.
And when I crashed and broke both lungs
on the wheel, you were so relieved
that you stroked the hard Ford paint
like a breast and your hands shook.

Twice More

understand me please there's no man underneath there's
no woman no dog no opening what happens in the first
place is hunger is silence a cold
mathematical thumb-mark and
every time I hurt I didn't mean it
and when the shame quit closing its little mouth locking
its feet down melting what happened
was that they didn't care they ticked
a night off they counted
me up they threw my name back

so understand me the long emblem of death is washed out
the famous scar cries but
if I wanted you I still would if I desired
I would if I cut the mistake down
there is a man with nothing in
him but blood there is a blank
gene drifting a bone with cells
in it and I am myself again I start
again I walk
in a storm of lost handfuls and tell them
and twice more I tell them and
twice more
I am myself again

On the Roof

The trouble with me is that whether I get love or not
I suffer from it. My heart always seems to be prowling
a mile ahead of me, and, by the time I get there to surround it,
it's chewing fences in the next county, clawing
the bank-vault wall down or smashing in the window
I'd just started etching my name on with my diamond.

And that's how come I end up on the roof. Because even if I talk
into my fist everyone still hears my voice like the ocean
in theirs, and so they solace me and I have to keep
breaking toes with my gun-boots and coming up here
to live—by myself, like an aerial, with a hand on the ledge,
one eye glued to the tin door and one to the skylight.

It Is This Way with Men

They are pounded into the earth
like nails; move an inch,
they are driven down again.
The earth is sore with them.
It is a spiny fruit
that has lost hope
of being raised and eaten.
It can only ripen and ripen.
And men, they too are wounded.
They too are sifted from their loss
and are without hope. The core
softens. The pure flesh softens
and melts. There are thorns, there
are the dark seeds, and they end.

Sleeping Over

FOR DAVE AND MARK ROTHSTEIN

There hasn't been any rain
since I arrived. The lawns
are bleached and tonight goldenrod
and burnt grass reflect
across my walls like ponds.
After all these days
the textures and scents of my room
are still strange and comforting.
The pines outside, immobile
as chessmen, fume turps
that blend with the soap taste
of the sheets and with the rot
of camphor and old newspapers
in the bare bureau drawers.
Jarred by a headlight's glare
from the country road, the crumbling
plaster swarms with shadows.
The bulb in the barn, dull
and eternal, sways and flickers
as though its long drool
of cobwebs had been touched,
and the house loosens, unmoors,
and, distending and shuddering, rocks
me until I fall asleep.

In December the mare
I learned to ride on died.
On the frozen paddock hill,
down, she moaned all night
before the mink farmers
came in their pickup
truck, sat on her dark
head and cut her throat.

I dream winter. Shutters
slamming apart. Bags
crammed with beer bottles
tipping against clapboard.
Owls in chimneys.
Drafts; thieves; snow.
Over the crusty fields
scraps of blue loveletters
mill wildly like children,
and a fat woman, her rough
stockings tattered away
at a knee, sprints in high,
lumbering bounds among
the skating papers. Out
to the road—red hydrant,
bus bench, asphalt—
a wasp twirling at her feet,
she is running back.

My first kiss was here.
I can remember the spot—
next to a path, to
a cabin, a garden patch—
but not how it happened
or what I felt, except
amazement that a kiss
could be soundless. Now,
propped on an elbow,
I smoke through the dawn, smudging
the gritty sheets with ashes,
wondering what if that night
someone nearby had snorted
aloud, had groaned or even
just rustled a branch.

Day finally. The trees
and fences clarify, unsnarl.
Flagstones, coins, splash

across the driveway crowns
and the stark underbrush
animals go away.
A rickety screen door bangs,
slaps its own echo
twice. There are no footsteps
but someone is out sifting
ashes in the garbage pit.
Suddenly dishes jangle
the bright middle distances
and the heat begins again:
by now the ground must be
hard and untillable as ice.
Far off from the house,
the lake, jellied with umber
weed scum, tilts toward
the light like a tin tray.
Dead rowboats clog
the parched timber dam
and along the low banks
the mounds of water rubble
I gathered yesterday
have dried and shrunk down
to a weak path wobbling
back and forth from the edge.

Three Seasons and a Gorilla

these americans just looking
you can tell their big toenails are
blue with welts running
across the base and pain
you can tell the pain miles
from here you can smell
it
and these frenchmen jesus
infections on
the hairline and what pain you need
the wind
but o god what wailing from each
follicle each
strand

and these asians
and these southamericans and
eskimos
think of the clogged pores
in the armpit and the
raw spots at the root
of the penis and the pimple that grows
inwards and shoots and
again again what
agony what cold misery coming
back hitting you in the neck what
stinking and take me
a big clothes-
bag the buttons
all crying the zippers
giving up the seams the torn
crotch lines groaning and just
think what pain god what
pain

The Other Side

Across the way hands
move nervously on curtains,
and behind them, radiated
with arc light, silver,
there is almost no face.
Almost no eyes look at me through this air.
Almost no mouth twists
and repeats, following my mouth, the shrill ciphers
that cross like swallows.

Tonight the breeze from the distillery
stinks of death. Do you think men have died
in the vats tonight? Everyone waits,
sick with the stench of mash
and spirits, and the tubs lick
their own sides with little splashes,
little bubbles that pop, clearing themselves.

In this breeze, it is strange to be telling myself,
Life, what are you saying?
In this breeze, almost like hands, words
climb on the thin gauze of curtains
and drop. Men float
from corner to corner, and, almost like hands,
birds put their sore wings under the eaves
and sleep.

Of What Is Past

I hook my fingers into the old tennis court fence
and kneel down in an overgrowth of sharp weeds
to watch the troopers in their spare compound drill.

Do you remember when this was a park? When girls
swung their rackets here in the hot summer mornings
and came at night to open their bodies to us?

Now gun-butts stamp the pale clay like hooves.
Hard boots gleam.
And still, children play tag and hide-and-seek

beyond the barriers. Lovers sag in the brush.
It's not them, it's us: we know too much.
Soon only the past will know what we know.

Ashes Ashes We All Fall Down

how come when grandpa is teaching the little boy
to sing he can't no matter what remember even
though he taps time hard with his teeth like a cricket even
though he digs in hard with his fingers how come?

and when he grows tall he will name everyone
he meets father or mother but will still have no songs
he leans back among the cold pages he falls down
in the palace of no sleep where the king cries and

in the new country the musical soldiers will
beat him he will sell silver consonants out
of his car the lady will cup his dry testicles
in the drone the soldiers beat him again

I miss you now can you
remember the words at least? and the
new name? when pain comes
you must kill it when beauty comes

with her smiles you must kill them I
miss you again I miss you white
bug I miss you sorrow rain radio I miss
you old woman in my bible in the dream

Trappers

In the dark with an old song
I sit, in the silence,
and it knows me
by heart and comes faltering
gently through me
like a girl in love,
in a room, evening,
feeling her way.

When good mountain men
were snowed in for months
in the Rockies, sleet
hissing over the sharp crust
to hollow places, branches
groaning through the night,
they must have done what I do
now, and been as terrified.

I let a word out,
and what comes, an awful drone,
a scab, bubbles up
and drills away unfadingly.
Later, in a place far
from here, feeling softly on her neck
like a fly, she will gaze
into the sunlight, and not see me.

Being Alone

Never on one single pore Eternity
have I been touched by your snows

or felt your shy mouth tremble,
your breath break on me

like the white wave. I have not felt
your nakedness tear me

with hunger or your silver hands
betray me but today I promise

whatever flower of your house
should bloom I will stay

locked to its breast.
Like little fish who live

harmlessly under the bellies of sharks,
I will go where you go,

drift inconspicuously
in the raw dredge of your power

like a leaf, a bubble of carrion,
a man who has understood and does not.

Trash

I am your garbage man. What you leave,
I keep for myself, burn or throw
on the dump or from scows in the delicious river.
Your old brown underpants are mine now,
I can tell from them
what your dreams were. I remember
how once in a closet with shoes
whispering and mothballs, you held on
and cried like a woman. Your nights stink
of putrid lampshades, of inkwells and silk
because my men and I with our trails
of urine and soft eggs and our long brooms
hissing, came close.

What do they do with kidneys and toes
in hospitals? And where did your old dog go
who peed on the rug and growled?
They are at my house now, and what grinds
in your wife's teeth while she sleeps
is mine. She is chewing
on embryos, on the eyes of your lover,
on your phone book and the empty glass
you left in the kitchen. And in your body,
the one who died there and rots
secretly in the fingers of your spirit,
she is hauling his genitals out, basket
after basket
and mangling all of it in the crusher.

Giving It Up

It is an age
of such bestial death
that even before we die
our ghosts go.
I have felt mine while I slept
send shoots over my face,
probing some future char
there, tasting the flesh
and the sweat
as though for the last time.

And I have felt him
extricate himself and go,
crying, softening himself
and matching his shape
to new bodies; merging,
sliding into souls,
into motors, buildings,
stop signs, policemen—
anything.

By morning, he is back.
Diminished, shorn
of his light, he lies crumpled
in my palm, shivering
under my breath like cellophane.
And every day
there is nothing to do
but swallow him like a cold
tear
and get on with it.

For Gail, When I Was Five

My soul is out back eating your soul.
I have you tied in threads like a spider
and I am drinking down your laughter
in huge spoonfuls. It is like tinsel.
It sprays over the crusty peach baskets
and the spades hung on pegs. It is like air
and you are screaming, or I am, and we are
in different places with wild animal faces.

What does God do to children who touch
in the darkness of their bodies and laugh?
What does he think of little underpants
that drift down on the hose like flowers?
God eats your soul, like me. He drinks
your laughter. It is God in the history
of my body who melts your laughter
and spits it in the wounds of my life like tears.

Don't

I have been saying what I have to say
for years now, backwards and forwards
and upside down and you haven't heard
it yet, so from now on
I'm going to start unsaying it:
I'm going to unsay what I've said already
and what everyone else has said
and what hasn't even been said yet.

I'm going to unsay
the northern hemisphere
and the southern,
east and west, up
and down, the good
and the bad. I'm going to unsay
what floats just over my skin
and just under: the leaves
and the roots, the worm
in the river and the whole river
and the ocean and the ocean
under the ocean. Space
and light are going,
silence, sound, flags,
photographs, dollar bills:
the sewer people and the junk people,
the money people and the concrete people
who ride out of town on dreams
and love it, and the dreams,
even the one pounding
under the floor like a drum—
I'm going to run them all down
again the other way
and end at the bottom.

Do you see? Caesar is unsaid
now. Christ
is unsaid. They trade toys
but it's too late.
The doctor is unsaid, cured;
the rubber sheet grows
leaves, luscious and dark,
and the patient feels them
gathering at the base
of his spine like a tail.
It is unsaid
that we have no tails—
an old lady twirls hers
and lifts
like a helicopter.

Time turns
backwards in its womb and floats out
in its unsaying.
It won't start again.
The sad physicist
throws switches but all
the bomb does is sigh inwardly
and hatch like an egg,
and little void-creatures
come, who live
in the tones between notes,
innocent and unstruck.

A baby fighting for air
through her mother's breast
won't anymore: the air is unsaid.
The skeleton I lost in France
won't matter. No picnics,
no flattened grass,
no bulls.

Everything washes up,
clean as morning.
My wife's wet underwear in the sink—
I unsay them,
they swallow me
like a Valentine.
The icebox is growing baby green
lima beans for Malcolm Lowry.
The house fills with love.
I chew perfume
and my neighbor kissing me good morning
melts and goes out
like a light.

There is bare rock
between here and the end.
There is a burnt place
in the silence.

Along my ribs, dying of old age,
the last atom dances
like a little girl. I unsay
her yellow dress, her hair,
her slippers
but she keeps dancing,
jumping back and forth
from my face to my funny bone
until I burst out laughing.

And then I unsay
the end.

Just Right

the way we get under cars and in
motors you'd think we were made for them our hands
slotting in the carbs our feet
on the pedals and how everything
even flowers even the horns of cattle fits
just right it is like nail and hole
even apples even hand grenades with indentations
for our fingers and the detonations patterns finding us
all this given and how ungrateful we are
dreaming that someday we won't touch anything
that all this space will close on us
the fire sprout through us and blossom and
the tides

dear father of the fire save me enough room please
and dear water-mother I'd like two clear drops
to float in brothers and sisters I'll need
your engines and computers I'll need four tall buildings
and heaters and strong-bulldozers with
thick treads and switches and there must be
uniforms
there must be maps and hoses and
tiled rooms to drain the blood off
and will your voices
come telling me you love me? and your mouths
and hands? and your cold
music? every inch of me? every
hour of me?

After That

Do you know how much pain is left
in the world? One tiny bit of pain is left,
braised on one cell like a toothmark.
And how many sorrows there still are? Three sorrows:
the last, the next to the last and this one.

And there is one promise left, feeling
its way through the poison, and one house
and one gun and one shout of agony
that wanders in the lost cities and the lost mountains.
And so this morning, suffering the third sorrow

from the last, feeling pain in my last gene,
cracks in the struts, bubbles in the nitro,
this morning for someone I'm not even sure exists
I waste tears. I count down by fractions
through the ash. I howl. I use up everything.

Or

Here's where I started
running from a little bee
is here now coated with soot his back legs
stuck together with black honey
black granules
on his jaws he speaks in my voice
he spreads his wings and something
budges in him but
not me

I'm here now

I found one day
without dying

I found it when everyone
except for one man
cursing kept
quiet everyone but one corpse
with gold

in its gullet

I found it when
when I said HANDS
I meant
your breasts when I said
SILENCE I meant
what never
touches

And did I come back?

I'm in eight pieces
like a toy truck
I'm in the mailbox I'm
in the cabin by the pond
I'm on the lawn

am I still
running?

I'm still running I'm still holding
everything together I'm still
me

I got there
where the lines met where
the laughter
opened the stones
desired something the slash mark
cried I got
there I got back I'm still
running nothing
comes in nothing
goes out I
see

Ten Below

It is bad enough crying for children
suffering neglect and starvation in our world
without having on a day like this
to see an old cart horse covered with foam,
quivering so hard that when he stops
the wheels still rock slowly in place
like gears in an engine.
A man will do that, shiver where he stands,
frozen with false starts,
just staring,
but with a man you can take his arm,
talk him out of it, lead him away.

What do you do when both hands
and your voice are simply goads?
When the eyes you solace see space,
the wall behind you, the wisp of grass
pushing up through the curb at your feet?
I have thought that all the animals
we kill and maim, if they wanted to
could stare us down, wither us
and turn us to smoke with their glances—
they forbear because they pity us,
like angels, and love of something else
is why they suffer us and submit.

But this is Pine Street, Philadelphia, 1965.
You don't believe
in anything divine being here.
There is an old plug with a worn blanket
thrown on its haunches. There is a wagon
full of junk—pipes and rotted sinks,
the grates from furnaces—and there

is a child walking beside the horse
with sugar, and the mammoth head lowering,
delicately nibbling from those vulnerable
fingers. You can't cut your heart out.
Sometimes, just what is, is enough.

Tails

there was this lady once she used to grow
snakes in her lap

they came up like tulips
from her underpants and the tops
of her stockings and she'd get us
with candy and have us pet
the damned things

god they were horrible skinned
snakes all dead
it turned out she'd catch
them in the garden and skin
them and drive
knitting needles up along the spines
and sew them on
it stank
the skins rotting in the corner heads
scattered all over the floor

it turned out she loved
children she wanted
to do something
for us we ate
the candy of course we touched
the snakes we
hung around god
we hated her she was
terrible

Sky, Water

FOR BRUCE AND FOX MCGREW

They can be fists punching the water—
muskrats, their whole bodies plunging
through weak reeds from the bank,
or the heads of black and white ducks
that usually flicker in quietly
and come up pointing heavenwards.

A man can lie off the brown scum of a slough
and watch how they'll go in like blades,
deeply, to the bottom,
and in his pale silence
with the long field furrows strumming
like distant music,
he will wonder at and pity
the creatures hooked together like flowers on the water,
who will die flashing in the air,
shaken in the beak of sunlight.

The surface tainted with small blood,
there can be bees and water hydra,
sea-grasses and blown seed,
and before a man's eyes life and death,
silence and the dim scream of love
can rise and furl up
from the bottom like smoke
and thin away.

Downwards

This is the last day of the world. On the river docks
I watch for the last time the tide get higher
and chop in under the stinking pilings. How the small creatures
who drift dreaming of hands and lungs must sting,
rotting alive in the waste spill, coming up dead
with puffy stomachs paler than the sky or faces.
There is deep fire fuming ash to the surface.
It is the last tide and the last evening and from now
things will strive back downwards.
A fish thrown up will gasp in the flare
and flop back hopelessly through the mud flats to the water.
The last man, an empty bottle with no message, is here, is me,
and I am rolling, fragile as a bubble in the upstream spin,
battered by carcasses, drawn down by the lips of weeds
to the terrible womb of torn tires and children's plastic shoes
and pennies and urine. I am no more, and what is left,
baled softly with wire, floating
like a dark pillow in the hold of the brown ship, is nothing.
It dreams. Touching fangs delicately with cranes
and forklifts, it rests silently in its heavy ripening.
It stands still on the water, rocking, blinking.

Shells

It's horrible, being run over by a bus
when all you are is a little box turtle.
You burst. Your head blasts out like a cork
and soars miles
to where the boy sprawls on the grass strip
beside the sidewalk. In mid-air
you are him. Your face touches his face,
you stutter, and you will go all your life
holding your breath,
wondering what you meant.

                                He forgets now
but he knew it in his cheek scorched
by the sweet blades and in his wild groin.
In his mother's arms, screaming,
he knew it: that he was crossing
under the laughter and there was the other voice
sobbing, It's not far, It's not far.

Beyond

Some people,
they just don't hate enough yet.
They back up, snarl, grab guns
but they're like children,
they overreach themselves;
they end up standing there feeling stupid,
wondering if it's worth it.

Some people, they don't have a cause yet.
They just throw their hate here and there
and sooner or later it's hollow
and they say, What is this?
and after that it's too late.
After that you can barely
button your sleeve in the morning—
you just take breaths.

Some people are too tired to hate
and so they think, Why live?
They read the papers, wince,
but they're hardly there anymore.
You go by them in the street
and they don't spit or mutter—
they look at themselves in store windows,
they touch their faces.

Some people, you give up
on them. You let them go,
you lose them.
They were like children, they hardly
knew what they meant. You think to yourself,
Good Riddance.

Saturday

I hate reading about dead men knowing
that in the end they cut him down
anyway and he went out screaming
for his wife in tears and I hate it also
about all the poor murderers in jail on their
birthdays what do they think about the rain
streaming the double doors the toilet
in the corner maybe they're sensitive they
want you to shit while they're asleep please
maybe they don't ever want to get up again
and people who are so proud
of their teeth they have mirrors over the bed
and a loudspeaker and they listen to them
clack clack all day what about them
he's thinking about ten thousand men
their arms over their heads their dirty
skirts flying all running at him turbans
sandals loose on the ground hands flapping
they have mustaches most
of them beards beautiful wrists and then
he thinks it's my birthday too and he goes
clack again clack clack and says
please not now it's raining my birthday
please one more day I hate this
the way he just shivers and doesn't do
anything the way the rain just keeps coming
the walls just
stand there
from now on I'm not saying it I'm going
to be saturday from now on and not
touch it there is a white flower there
is a postmark that's all

Patience Is When You Stop Waiting

I stand on the first step under the torn mouths of hours
in a new suit. Terrified of the arched webs and the dust,
of my speech, my own hair slicked with its thin pride,
I jut like a thorn; I turn, my pain turns and closes.

Tell me again about silence. Tell me I won't,
not ever, hear the cold men whispering in my pores
or the mothers and fathers who scream in the bedroom
and throw boxes of money between them and kiss.

At the window, faces hover against the soft glow
like names. If I cry out, it will forget me and go;
if I don't, nothing begins again. Tell me
about mercy again, how she rides in eternity's arms

in the drifts and the dreams come. The night is dying.
Wisely it thinks of death as a thing born of desire.
Gently it opens its sharp ribs and bites through
and holds me. Tell me about my life again, where it is now.

Faint Praise

FOR JIM MOSS, 1935–1961

Whatever last slump of flesh
rolls like a tongue in the mouth of your grave,
whatever thin rags of your underwear
are melting in slow, tiny stomachs,
I am still here; I have survived.

I thought when you died that your angels,
stern, dangerous bats with cameras and laws,
would swarm like bees
and that the silences flaming from you
would fuse me like stone.

There were no new landscapes I could prepare for you.
I let you go.
And tonight, again, I will eat, read,
and my wife and I will move into love
in the swells of each other like ships.
The loose aerial outside will snap,
the traffic lights blink and change,
the dried lives of autumn crackle like cellophane.

And I will have my life still.
In the darkness, it will lie over against me,
it will whisper, and somehow,
after everything, open to me again.

Halves

I am going to rip myself down the middle into two pieces
because there is something in me that is neither
the right half nor the left half nor between them.
It is what I see when I close my eyes, and what I see.

As in this room there is something neither ceiling
nor floor, not space, light, heat or even
the deep skies of pictures, but something that beats softly
against others when they're here and others not here,

that leans on me like a woman,
curls up in my lap and walks
with me to the kitchen or out of the house altogether
to the street—I don't feel it, but it beats and beats;

so my life: there is this, neither before me
nor after, not up, down, backwards nor forwards from me.
It is like the dense, sensory petals in a breast
that sway and touch back. It is like the mouth of a season,

the cool speculations bricks murmur, the shriek in orange,
and though it is neither true nor false, it tells me
that it is quietly here, and, like a creature, is in pain;
that when I ripen it will crack open the locks, it will love me.

Penance

I only regret the days wasted in no pain.
I am sorry for having touched bottom
and loved again.
I am sorry for the torn sidewalks
and the ecstasy underneath, for the cars,
the old flower-lady watching her fingers,
my one shoe in the morning
with death on its tongue.

In the next yard a dog whines
and whines for his lost master
and for the children who have gone
without him. I am sorry
because his teeth click on my neck,
because my chest shudders and the owl cries
in the tug of its fierce sacrament.

I repent God and children,
the white talons of peace and my jubilance.
Everything wheels
in the iron rain, smiling and lying.
Forgive me, please.

It Is Teeming

In rain like this what you want is an open barn door
to look out from. You want to see the deep hoofprints
in the yard fill and overflow, to smell the hay and hear
the stock chewing and stamping and their droppings pattering.

Of course the messengers would come away. A wet mutt,
his underlip still crisp with last night's chicken blood
will drift through the gate and whine and nuzzle
your knee with a bad look like a secret drinker,

and you will wish for the lions, the claws that erected
and slashed back, because you are tired of lording it,
of caving ribs in, of swinging axes and firing.
Where are the angels with trucks who pulled the trees down?

Now it is pure muck, half cowshit, half mud and blood, seething.
You have to go out back, dragging it, of course. No one
sees you with it. The rain—you throw wakes up like a giant.
The way you wanted it, the way it would be, of course.

From Now On

FOR MURRAY DESSNER

this knowledge so innocently it goes this sin
it dies without looking back it ripens
and dissolves and behind it behind
january behind bread and trenches there
are rooms with no gods in them there are breasts
with no deaths anymore and no promises
I knew mercy would leave me and turn
back I knew things in their small nests would
want me and say Come and things blossoming
say Go Downwards but still am I no bigger
than one man? not a pint more? a
watt? a filament of pity or sweetness? I turn
over first one side heads and then tails
I love life first then death first I
close I open I split down like an amoeba
into bricks and sunrise and longing
but we are suffering seven directions at once
the mouths in our mouths don't tell us
the sorrowful faces in our tears not
touch us nothing holds us nothing reaps
us we are not lived we are not suffered
the dreams come for us but they fail

A Day for Anne Frank

I

I look onto an alley here
where, though tough weeds and flowers thrust up
through cracks and strain
toward the dulled sunlight,
there is the usual filth spilling from cans,
the heavy soot shifting in the gutters.
People come by mostly
to walk their dogs or take the shortcut
between the roaring main streets,
or just to walk
and stare up at the smoky windows,
but this morning when I looked out
children were there running back and forth
between the houses toward me.
They were playing with turtles—
skimming them down the street
like pennies or flat stones,
and bolting, shouting, after the broken corpses.
One had a harmonica, and as he ran,
his cheeks bloating and collapsing like a heart,
I could hear its bleat, and then the girls' screams
suspended behind them with their hair,
and all of them: their hard, young breath,
their feet pounding wildly on the pavement to the corner.

2

I thought of you at that age.
Little Sister, I thought of you,
thin as a door,

and of how your thighs would have swelled
and softened like cake,
your breasts have bleached
and the new hair growing on you like song
would have stiffened and gone dark.
There was rain for a while, and then not.
Because no one came, I slept again,
and dreamed that you were here with me,
snarled on me like wire,
tangled so closely to me that we were vines
or underbrush together,
or hands clenched.

3

They are cutting babies in half on bets.
The beautiful sergeant has enough money to drink
for a week.
The beautiful lieutenant can't stop betting.
The little boy whimpers
he'll be good.
The beautiful cook is gathering up meat
for the dogs.
The beautiful dogs
love it all.
Their flanks glisten.
They curl up in their warm kennels
and breathe.
They breathe.

4

Little Sister,
you are a clot
in the snow,
blackened,
a chunk of phlegm
or puke

and there are men with faces
leaning over you with watercans

watering you!
in the snow, as though flowers would sprout
from your armpits
and genitals.

Little Sister,
I am afraid of the flowers sprouting from you

I am afraid of the silver petals
that crackle
of the stems darting
in the wind
of the roots

5

The twilight rots.
Over the greasy bridges and factories,
it dissolves
and the clouds swamp in its rose
to nothing.
I think sometimes the slag heaps by the river
should be bodies
and that the pods of moral terror
men make of their flesh should split
and foam their cold, sterile seeds into the tides
like snow
or ash.

6

Stacks of hair were there
little mountains
the gestapo children must have played in

and made love in and loved
the way children love haystacks or mountains

O God the stink
of hair oil and dandruff

their mothers must have thrown them into their tubs
like puppies and sent them to bed

coming home so filthy stinking

of jew's hair

of gold fillings, of eyelids

7

Under me on a roof
a sparrow little by little
is being blown away.
A cage of bone is left,
part of its wings,
a stain.

8

And in Germany the streetcar conductors go to work
in their stiff hats,
depositing workers and housewives
where they belong,
pulling the bell chains,
moving drive levers forward or back.

9

I am saying goodbye to you before our death. Dear Father:
I am saying goodbye to you before my death. We are so

anxious to live, but all is lost—we are not allowed! I am
so afraid of this death, because little children are thrown
into graves alive. Goodbye forever.
                         I kiss you.

10

Come with me Anne.
Come,
it is awful not to be anywhere at all,
to have no one
like an old whore,
a general.

Come sit with me here
kiss me; my heart too is wounded
with forgiveness.

There is an end now.
Stay.
Your foot hooked through mine
your hand against my hand
your hip touching me lightly

it will end now
it will not begin again

Stay
they will pass
and not know us

the cold brute earth
is asleep

there is no danger

there is nothing

Anne

there is nothing

I Am
the Bitter
Name

I Am the Bitter Name

And Abraham said to him, "And art thou, indeed,
he that is called Death?"
He answered, and said, "I am the Bitter Name."

the little children have been fighting
a long long time for their beloved country
their faces are hardening like meat
left out their bodies squashed flat
like flowers in lawbooks don't fit
with the keys to eternal sorrow anymore
is the best toy always death? everyone
crying in the sleepy hair inexhaustible
agony in the dark cups of the skull
unquenchable agony your hands shriek
on my spine like locked brakes in
the torn nostrils tendrils in the mouth
vines the little soldiers play
wounding the little generals play hurt
forever they sharpen things they put
things in things they pull them out
will you make freedom for me? in
the cheekbone fire in the lips my
justice is to forget being here my liberty
wanting to hate them how they are shipped
home in ice-cream bags and being able to

Keep It

the lonely people are marching
on the capital everyone's yelling not
to give them anything but just
buying dinner together was fun
wasn't it? don't give them a thing
the boss said the boss
is dreaming of beautiful nurses
the lonely people are taking
all their little dogs to washington
back home the channels change
by themselves the soap changes
to perfume perfume to cereal the boss
dreams of the moon landing on
spruce street nobody is lonely
on locust nobody is left
at all the sun comes by himself
the buses go along by themselves
and wonder have I told you about
my disease? the lonely people
hold tight at night
on the coast they are tucked
in under the twilight
together the boss walks
across them it was fun it was
so much fun wasn't it?

The Spirit the Triumph

do you remember learning to tie your shoes?
astonishing! the loops you had to make the delicate
adjustments the pulling-through tightening impossible!
the things we learn!
putting a bridle on a horse when he's head-shy
getting your hands under a girl's sweater
no wonder we are the crown of all that exists
we can do anything how we climb chimneys
how we put one foot on the gas one on the clutch
and make the car go nothing too difficult nothing!

crutches artificial arms have you seen that?
how they pick their cups up and use razors? amazing!
and the wives shine it for them at night
they're sleeping the wives take it out of the room
and polish it with its own special rag
it's late they hold it against their bellies
the leather laces dangle into their laps
the mechanisms slip noiselessly
lowering the hook softly onto their breasts
we men! aren't we something? I mean
we are worth thinking about aren't we?
we are the end we are the living end

How Humble We Were Before This

what if the ethical gunmen isolated evil
out of death and all there was left was screaming
I hate you at each other the targets
licked clean the ground white as aspirin we weren't
sacrificed to the golden sorrow we didn't win
prizes for suffering did we? I
am so sorry for us picture
this you are dragging me
through the front lines your velvety guts
string out on wires your face transfigures
with concentration but I come back
I cry harder and echoes how
are you what's new kiss me fuck me love
me are there anyway right? ponies
with scarlet shoulders right? prisoners
lullabying our sore breath with ashes?
everything we left out everything
we were afraid of is jammed back
in us like gigantic numbers swollen
with wanting killing with wanting being
alive without killing but always vengeance
I nail the dimes back I bite harder
than dear life what it is to be empty
what it is without passion there
is nothing like this being sanctified

Madder

"People can screw dead bodies, but they never feed them."

the nations have used up their desire
the cunts of the mothers the cunts
of the bad daughters stinking
of police stations of the sisters
and generations of men saying
look cunt what about me saying look
cunt how I'm bleeding saying cunt cunt
where is forgiveness? what bullshit

you can kiss me goodbye but first put
your hands up let me search you
first goodbye I'll check your rectum
for poison and recite how we spoiled
from the inside like lettuce I'll tell
about freedom vomited on our foreheads
I'll say LOOK WHAT YOU DID and men
reading money aloud laughing aloud

I'm fed up with the sugars of raw
human flesh cursing I gallop over her
with my nicked tongue head to toe
I plow in with my notched cock cursing
the suffering of labels the
suffering of elegant canned goods of
mercy vengeance witness borne
for no end the governments are silent

or I'm dying of grief and loving both
ends of it or of solace and mixing
up whether we're here at all and revenge
or peace and who did it first dear
husbands dear wives tighter they're

washing my mouth out with soap I promise
not to accuse you but this time you
be the secret this time you comfort me

Poor Hope

which is worse the lieutenant raising his rifle
toward the astonished women and children jammed
into the bomb crater raising it not even aiming just carelessly
beginning to do it the way you'd rake a lawn you start
anywhere that or when I saw a boy in a department store
with his mother he was skipping along going toot toot toot
when the mother saw me I could see her flinch about something
and when I passed them she cracked him him! not me
across the mouth stunning him terribly hissing
don't you know where you are? which is worse
to be in the world with that or with that? or is it
that there's god and you think they've killed him!
then the dread god did you really say hit them! kill them!
then to the children then the mothers forgive me then myself then
nothing no sacrament for the people forgotten
in mid-sentence gone except in fuck you! where they cry god
I have thought two ways up the first
is when I felt the boy's spirit become pain because of me
I should have apologized not to him or even the mother
but to YOU! I'm sorry and the other is for the others
in the ditch in their torn clothes just as the bullets go into them
I would go mad and have you seen how men in toilets
at stadiums or the movies stare into the wall
so we won't covet each other's cocks? I would stare
into you like that and never move again never let you die
again never let you be anywhere else staring watching
you boil helplessly back and forth on the ceiling
don't move! trying to electrocute yourself on the wires
stay where you are! trying to slice your body
to pieces on the fluttering cobwebs don't die on me!

Bringing It Home

a room all the way across america
and a girl in the room and the plastic fattening her breasts
starting to sag o god
she thinks they're going o god o god
I would do anything to help her
I would take all of her secret pain onto myself if she'd let me
my best darling
it is your soul melting it
it is the fire in you

I remember fire
everywhere in the world
boys scratching two sticks together so proud of themselves
houses going up in spontaneous combustion or somebody using
     his lighter
and the girl locked in in back still touching her fearful body
(you too my best darling)
and furnaces men with sweat stung out of them
faces cooked broiled smoked while they make things for us

and in america
in her breasts the two fires
like gods the two fires without flame
and her voice this flame rising out of my throat
it says FUCK YOU I DON'T CARE
it says UP YOUR ASS TOO YOU WEIRD FAGGOTS
my best darling my best darling

The Little Shirt

what we need is one of those gods
who comes howling down streets
like a police car into the houses into
the television sets the refrigerators
comes oozing through everything and eats
everything everything the whole box
the darkness the dust
under the stairs the roaches and then us
and then makes us up again
out of her wonderful mouth earth
so that we look into our friends suddenly understanding
flesh how it tightens and lets go
to have this pass through
to be able to blink so that it goes through
to be able to get back from this
so mother death will be happy
so we won't hurt her she
keeps her big hand on us her thighs over our heads
she jumps we fall out like apples
and having to own her
and having to have war for her and fucking
and thankfulness so she won't stink in her people
we believe her
cloudlife airlife scent the
flavors to lick off
going up firing back at ourselves
make me sergeant! get me a hard-on!
to kill
never to go from this

Clay out of Silence

chances are we will sink quietly back
into oblivion without a ripple
we will go back into the face
down through the mortars as though it hadn't happened

earth: I'll remember you
you were the mother you made pain
I'll grind my thorax against you for the last time
and put my hand on you again to comfort you

sky: could we forget?
we were the same as you were
we couldn't wait to get back sleeping
we'd have done anything to be sleeping

and trees angels for being thrust up here
and stones for cracking in my bare hands
because you foreknew
there was no vengeance for being here

when we were flesh we were eaten
when we were metal we were burned back
there was no death anywhere but now
when we were men when we became it

Innings

somebody keeps track of how many times
I make love don't you god don't you?
and how good it is telling me
it's marked down where I can't see
right underneath me so the next time
something unreal happens in the papers
I don't understand it it doesn't touch
me I start thinking
everyone's heart might be pure
after all because what the hell
they don't kill me just each other
they don't actually try making me sad
just do things make things happen
suffer things I erupt
into the feminine like a lion don't
I god? among doves? so even being with me
is like beauty? I move under this god
like a whore I gurgle I roll
like a toy boat what's the score
now god? am I winning?

Creams

put mommy on the front steps
with her legs open and baby all
grown up hers too every morning
they'd tangle their pants off
and go out crying every
morning the soldiers
would be there washing themselves
like socks and the good part
would be breezes licking
in sparrows packed up in cartons
but the bad part again after
all this the children born
with self-addressed tags HOME
DARLING MY SORROW lashing
them like wings their voices
hurting them their hearts
trying to quench the hideous
laughter forgive
us we were alone for a long
time like this nothing would tell
us what was wrong and it
was delicious anyway being
blamed wanting to want too
much and being banged back
to the life again we tried
everything sweethearts we tried
the last thing and then this
death by itself then this

Becoming Somebody Else

your lists of victims dear
god like rows of sharp little teeth
have made me crazy look
I have crushed my poor balls
for you I have kissed the blank
pages drunk the pissy chalice
water and thrown up dear god your
rabbits dear god your big
whistle do you know how awful
it is trying to plug the holy wound
in my bowels with wrong addresses?
listen let us have death back
when we need him the lost mother
of bliss will sing in the back
seat for you let us come back
with our SS and our own banks
this time and for the corpses
compilers to start out dear concerned
chosen esteemed sufferer warm
gloves god our bodies ladders
lovely look we smile too this
way look our blood too touch us is
it horrible? touch us

Hounding Mercy

our poor angel how sick
he must be of burying his face
in our hot mouths breathing
in maggots and fruity lung tissue
puffing us up when all we do
is empty again the prayers
to the forbidden father stinking
on us like exhaust fumes the candles
stuck guttering in our backsides
suppose though we took your gun in one
hand your excellent scalpel behind
it and kept saying kiss kiss kiss kiss
and before they screamed we'd cut
them before they begged us blast
them and cannibalize them all legs
from one ethics from another somebody's
skull we'd suture until there was
one whole one and who'd need war
or politics would the mothers kill
their beautiful children from sheer
boredom the fathers fight
over the fucked carcasses like sharks?
here is my magic briefcase
which roars here the branch
of my life to beat it with my
handcuffs what will I want now? give
me love give me snow oceans don't speak

What Did the Man Do with the Clouds?

the grandmas are all coming down like f-101's like gulls
screaming HAPPIER! HAPPIER! the grandmas
loom along the parapets like old wars their
grooved bellies grenades the lines kissed
into their faces like barbed wire
grandmas I've got the wings you brought me but they won't work
for me they don't fit anywhere on me
except in my mouth I keep sticking them
onto me like matchbooks but brother adam moses the pope
I don't see anyone the grandmas are all laughing
on the back fence like cold soup grandmas
if I could I'd wind myself onto you like a ribbon
and flow out behind you and be wind be sunrise
the grandmas bagpipe out of their soft wombs like apples
and go up like autumn in long rows like pearls like pearls
goodbye grandmas goodbye again thanks
for my present I swallowed them they're flapping
around inside me like uncle sol in the last chair
maybe someday they'll lift me like you
by the top of my guts out of here goodbye
charlie! go to sleep! eat! you're skin and bones! goodbye! goodbye!

The Matter

there's no no like money's
money makes big holes behind its eyes
when it says no and death
is the next teller
counting you money arches
and peeks down at the caseworker in the spirit drawer
money comes takes your picture without cameras
digs inside without shovels
smiles puts its head in the tube
like a robber
like the anchorite in the cave
like ten dollars
inside money is no candy but her
inside money no rate but just him
the prostitute without her vagina the brother
who wants you to money says no
and the last dollar
which is our friend dog
our history like a condom
lion
king
speaker
is dragged under and riveted
to the bone
like old age

Refuge, Serpent-Riders

a man decided once to go steal truth
all day he would tie himself to his bed
and not listen
at night the ropes would come off
he would go out and open his mouth
tasting what leaked through the moon from the next sky
rolling the stars around in his teeth
like little pits
finally darkness got tired of hanging there
it said how much will you give me? give me
something
the man started getting younger when he heard that
soon he was crawling the rocks
cut his knees he was really sorry
everybody else screamed BEAST FIEND MURDERER!
they pissed up into his maw
they named their lips death
so when they cried it would break in two pieces
then darkness went back
the stories still hid inside him it was morning
nobody had him
he still knew everything

Flat

the pillows are going insane
they are like shells the skulls have risen out of them like locusts
leaving faces in them but cold vacant immobile
heavy with tears
they are like clouds and are so sick of us
so furious with us they swear next time
when we come back if they can they will spring up and our
     faces will empty
next time they will soar like clouds and dissolve
and not touch us it is morning
our heads thrown back in agony

the pillows are going insane
from the grief of being laid down
and having to stare unquestioningly like flowers
and be in all places like flowers each man one in his house
one in his barracks in his jail cell
they swear if they weren't going insane they would call to each
     other
like flowers and spring up and come closer
but they must stay quietly
they must have faces like men and wait like men
the dead casings the filling and emptying going insane

The Admiral Fan

FOR TOM PALMORE

"The imagination of man's heart is evil from his youth . . ."

behind the barn the lady from the city
hikes her girdle up over her white backside
and into her before she knows it all the cows go all
the sheep the chickens geese old mule nannygoat
then o my god all over her breasts so many breasts
we have to make dolls to empty her
but the lobbyist of the dolls would come in his long car
wouldn't he? they are using her in washington
the country gets thin like an old woman
and they are bringing her back to me blubbering
armfuls ripped fabrics bubbles she is sobbing
against me my wife my
nation
the breasts were
dawn amity peace exaltation
in the fields the corn withering tomato vine bean vine
nothingness nothingness this
we flash upon like stoplights

A Poem for the Governments

this poem is an onion
it's the same one miguel hernandez'
wife wrote him about in jail
before he died that there was nothing
else for her and the baby to eat
except onions so he wrote
a lullaby for the child about onions
"I awoke from being a child:
don't you awake . . . don't even know
what happens or what goes on"

this poem is an onion
for you mr old men because
I want tears from you now
and can't see how else to get them
I want tears for miguel now
for the poor people and their children
and for the kids you hate going
around cunt-frontwards full of carrying on
and bad shit like mercy and despair
I offer this

because everything else with life
and tenderness in it you've eaten
everything good in the world eaten
everything in my heart eaten
the poor eaten the babies eaten miguel
eaten
now eat this: this is one onion
your history and legacy
it is all there is in our lives
this and tears: eat this

Another Dollar

I dreamed of an instrument of political torture
so that the person thinks he's breathing into a great space
that flows like a river beyond men
into infinity the ethical disconnects like a phone
and what he says everything comes back to him WE ARE NOT
    DOING THIS
angels skulls prisoners WE ARE NOT DOING THIS
the children scouring themselves like genitals NOT DOING THIS

mother am I the enemy or the little brother?
they threw ropes around me I ran I covered myself
but they touched me the invalids licked me the poor kissed me
afterwards there is a bed afterwards a woman is there
her breasts she is a cloud how she envelops you
the coils shimmer nobody talks anymore nobody dreams this
WE ARE NOT DOING THIS

The Beginning of April

I feel terribly strong today
it's like the time I arm-wrestled a friend
and beat him so badly I sprained his wrist
or when I made a woman who was really beautiful
love me when she didn't want to
it must be the warm weather
I think
I could smash bricks with my bare hands
or screw
until I was half out of my mind

the only trouble
jesus the only trouble
is I keep thinking about a kid I saw starving on television
last night from biafra he was unbearably fragile
his stomach puffed up arms and legs sticks eyes distorted
what if I touched somebody like that when I was this way?
I can feel him going stiff under my hands
I can feel his belly bulging ready to pop
his pale hair disengaging from its roots like something awful
   and alive
please

I won't hurt you I want you in my arms
I want to make something for you to eat like warm soup
look I'll chew the meat for you first
in case your teeth ache
I'll keep everybody away if you're sleeping
and hold you next to me like a little brother when we go out
I'm so cold now
what are we going to do with all this?
I promise I won't feel myself like this ever again
it's just the spring it doesn't mean anything please

This Is a Sin

right off we started inflicting history
on each other day after day first thing this
is historical and we gave dollars for it
and this and we gave movies and sad poems
and obviously newspapers and a little less
valentines and sometimes it got right
up against us and into us we would squeeze
it out like a worm it would come back
by itself through the pancreas through
the eye or womb and with great tenderness
on the faces of wives and babies we
would reinflict it until there was
such beauty it was unbearable because
it was too much history too much suffering
and also birds suffering their leaps
from branches dogs
lifting their dark mouths the paths
of mantises cows plopping were we afraid
of what would be left of us? sometimes
a person was erased entirely
and children dead of shame stuck
upright in the snow like pipes the wind
screaming over them or I would forget
you darling your breasts the wind
over them our lips
moving darling the child the wind breasts
our lips over them

The Undead

the only way it makes sense
is that we have terrible wounds inside us like mouths hard
metallic made in america
they swing fatly open like wallets and gorge
in strict vaginal contractions what touches us
what comes to us living wants us

how many times the one we kiss with affirms LIFE! LIFE!
but the other when the saints said
they heard thunder it was just it closing and
this time when it opens corpses soar in it officers
at attention shells
this time not enough pain in all asia for it

I want you not comforting me
the soles of our feet beaten until worms of flesh erupt from them
our genitals dialed like wrong numbers don't
put your tongue in me don't give me anything heart
soul laughter anything children turning the light on and off
on and off MA! don't feed me! don't feed me!

What Must I Do to Be Lost?

what I am now is the cock
of some infinite animal stiffening
and softening like a planet
in the spaces beyond kiss
before he had me
my animal pushed his face into the end and kept going
life rode him there
was no one he hadn't torn to pieces
my animal clicks back and forth and smokes
he wants to go through us now out of the universe
like both moons
he wants to cough into the sanctuaries bleed
on the risers shrivel
the fruits of our soul in his centuries
love pony darling let
me be fields mines dry ditches
my animal opens I
sway I thrust aimlessly nothing
is mine here
take the knife I can't here
swim in the thick break
me darling
I am nailed in like a root
meat

Then the Brother of the Wind

there's no such thing as death everybody
knows that also
nothing in the world that can batter you
and hang you on a fencepost like a towel

and no such thing as love that stays inside
getting thicker and heavier falling
into the middle one seed
that weighs more than the universe

and no angels either
and even if there were even if we hadn't laughed
the second heart out and made the second brain
have whole wars happening inside it like bacteria

and if they were made out of tin cans like shacks
in rio and rubber tires like crete sandals
and were all the same place rags in ratholes
in harlem rags sticking to burned faces in bengal

we'd still break like motors
and slip out of them anyway like penises
onto the damp thigh
and have to begin over

Like Little Birds

I'm sick and tired of sharing
everything with everybody I want a number of my own now
like god has with his name just me knowing it nobody
else unless I tell them
it's why there's money isn't it? we get a pile
start counting finish get
another still
wrong like god and the letters he puts death
onto life then life on top then love mixes them up throws them
    down
shuffles them picks them up one at a time then handfuls
bleeding

god what
I'll do now is lie down here and count backwards
and you'll tell me when
right? but god not
before zero this time it's dark
here you can't see
it's like a coffin things crawl in with you
take nibbles but you don't feel them
my poor number god I don't care
for myself but family friends government god
for their sake not here again

The Next to the Last Poem about God

when jessie's fever went up god got farther away so he could see
    better
he wanted to know everything that happened
when I hit tex my brother in the face with a cap gun
when I ran away from my mother and had a bad fight
with my sister lynn about being different
when I dreamed of being a fighter pilot and shooting my father down
god was there in my dream too think how big he had to be
to get in where I was sailing around in my flying tiger
and the deaf kid he was in his ears somebody told me so it was all
    right
and jimmy moss when he died it was autumn there were leaves
outside the window just hardening I thought
he must be in the leaves too how big he is how far away
he must be to cover everything like a blanket
you crawl in with a fever and hide and wake up some time
during the night all better and crawl out again
but maybe when he has to get that far he thins out a little
you know? like rubber? maybe sometimes people punch
their fingers through him by accident or maybe on purpose
the bad people because they wanted to see everything too
because seeing everything would be like owning everything
so they go through and there they were bouncing around
saying everything's good everything figures it all works
you could see them walking across the sky
at night rippling the cover making the stars bend
they said come up here look you can see EVERYTHING! EVERY-
    THING!
tex I'm sorry I hit you in the face
mom I didn't mean to grow up you should have told me lynn
dad forgive me for getting stronger
sally you for so much and jessie
when you were playing on the bed last night
letting yourself fall backwards onto me with such happy trust

thinking "stand up" meant "let yourself fall any way you want to
I'll catch you" jessie you were almost well your fever
was almost gone and I thought there must be something important
for you like that I still can't think of it but god must know it
because god doesn't forget anything ever
and someday I'll get that far too and find out
and drop messages about what it was and it'll be all right
god told me he said tell jessie I said it'll be all right

Acids

FOR JEFF MARKS

something to dip myself into
like sheep when they're driven through
and the ticks and fleas float off in the trough
the animals struggling to keep their heads out of it
the men dunking them for their own good they get fatter the
   wool thicker
I would come up
crying
but pure again fingerprints kissmarks the places
I crossed my arms and dug into my back invisible
scales imperceptible bony emotional excrescences
gone a caul
gleaming flushing the surfaces innocence
I would make rivers of it
that would flood at their mouths
and the swimmers
would be done too
and in the city in the tap water
enough scum left to get into us all
we would fall into great laughing heaps of ourselves
can you imagine laughter
shining
and the sounds of lovemaking
etched like printing plates
so you would pull pictures of being young and knowing
what you know now
the first sky the first clouds
like young angels
bumping each other seeing your mother coming shrieking
joyfully so she'll hear you
and come running arms open face open baby!
baby!
and you

flowing being flowed through
like the blood
over the skull then
the veil and before that in your arms
in all of you

They Warned Him Then They Threw Him Away

there's somebody who's dying
to eat god
when the name happens
the juices leap from the bottom of his mouth like waves
he almost falls over with lightheadedness
nobody has ever been this hungry before
you might know people who've never had anything
but teaspoons of rice or shreds
from the shin of an ape well that's nothing
you should know what this person would do
he'd pull handfuls of hair out of his children
and shove them down
he'd squeeze the docile bud in his wife
until it screamed
if you told him god lived in his own penis
he'd bite into it
and tear like a carnivore
this is how men renounce
this is how we obliterate
one morning near the end he'll climb into the fire
and look back at himself
what was dark will be light
what was song will be roaring
and the worst thing is you'll still want this
beyond measure you'll still want this
believe me
you should know this

Portions of Manslayer

my face ends inside you
it goes in on the tip
I am rushing into it
from behind where my back is
in the darkness and I want
to be this close nothing between us
the stripes burn there are just wisps
I go through where they were time
washes me like clear water and you
are in my face
inside too
but you say SAVE ME
you say GO BACK
well
this stinks
this face
the world is inside this face but it's lousy
remember you used to say MAKE A FACE
MAKE A FACE
for you
only
in the blood where you can't tell anyway
I'm making them
I whisper look! look!
but there's no world
I'm not in this face not this one
it stinks
it's just nothing

Jetsam

I'm being punished this time for crying
too much and because I used to inflict
pain on everybody I loved without knowing
it and so everything's finished the carburetor
I carried around tuning the single flower
the sink tap the window starting to murmur
where's charity? I can't think
of anything but the words for you bar
bedpost house I keep disappearing
in the holes where my voice was and
what I have by myself now this tube
in my left hand this meat in my tearing
right nobody knows
but the last man with rubbers pulled down
over his face who's me too it's night
his eyelids stop tears from
both ways so if somebody cried out loud
he'd call it compassion if there was nothing
ever again he'd say that's right desire

Ribbons

the goddamned animals might know more than we do about some
   things
like looking away when somebody they know is hurting them
and the other has to let go and not tear his throat out like us
but we're still more than them about love
a girl so shy she couldn't look at me without crying
so I turned the other way too and you could feel how close we were
as though we'd circled the whole world
and met and fallen in love her legs smoothed
I was stronger there were mists we walked in them

now when does that happen with pigs or horses?
the stallion all he's after is tearing the fence down
the mare gets her tail going like a pump handle
and in the paddock the gelding old sergeant
buries his face in the creaky feed bin and keeps it there
remembering iwo jima remembering the bulge seoul my lai
his wound his two thighs like medals his two thighs
rising into the dark like searchlights only animals would keep quiet
   then
grind their broad teeth on the grain and shut up not us

The Nut

a man hammers viciously
viciously like fucking
a bad whore who won't get
undressed even remember?
like trying to crush
the life from the corpse who
sprays blood who won't
die or stop screaming
until the mouth is gone
utterly the last thread
crawling tenderly down
the backbone tenderly
to the tail the legs men
what are we thinking
hammering? the poor whore
smashing her fists on
the wall the carpenter his
sensitive tools suffering
men the terrible claws
men the hammering not
sleeping the hammering
going on to eternity
what is this so much
like pulse like murdering?
the corpse screams the
woman screams men what
is this?

Yours

I'd like every girl in the world to have a poem of her own
I've written for her I don't even want to make love to them all
    anymore
just write things your body makes me delirious your face
    enchants me
you are a wonder of soul spirit intelligence one for every one
and then the men I don't care whether I can still beat them all
them too a poem for them how many?
seeing you go through woods like part of the woods seeing you
    play piano
seeing you hold your child in your tender devastating hands
and of course the children too little poems they could sing or
    dance to
this is our jumping game this our seeing game our holding each other
even the presidents with all their death the congressmen and judges
I'd give them something
they would hold awed to their chests as their proudest life thing
somebody walking along a road where there's no city would
    look up
and see his poem coming down like a feather out of nowhere
or on the assembly line new instructions a voice sweet as
    lunch-time
or she would turn over a stone by the fire and if she couldn't
    read
it would sing to her in her body
listen! everyone! you have your own poem now
it's yours as much as your heart as much as your own life is
you can do things to it shine it up iron it dress it in doll clothes
o men! o people! please stop how it's happening now please
I'm working as fast as I can I can't stop to use periods
sometimes I draw straight lines on the page because the words
are too slow

I can only do one at a time don't die first please
don't give up and start crying or hating each other they're coming
I'm hurrying be patient there's still time isn't there? isn't there?

The Nickname of Hell

the president of my country his face flushed
horribly like a penis is walking through
the schoolyard toward my daughter I tell him
mr president I will make it all right but
under his hand his penis is lined with many
buttons I tell him the orders are changing
but commanders deep in his penis prime it
I tell him about love I tell him there
is a new god who believes anything I
cringe alongside him I dance like a daughter
it is the schoolyard the daughters play
on the dangerous fences I tell him I love
him I tell him the daughters aren't here
even he is holding me now his arms hold
me his lips you are my bliss he tells me
these are my arms these my lips you
are my penis he tells me his face stings
into mine like a penis you are my joy you
my daughter hold me my daughter my daughter

The Kingdom
of Stinking Wishes

how is it some of us don't believe
about evil that it's only a little
of it you're not supposed to get
wrought up poor babies we
never heard mommy telling us
inside we heard her piss fizzing
like champagne but no secrets
and the daddies poor babies
what did they know all scurvied
up like underwear from working
so hard they heard the heroes
scrabbling under their shields
like roaches they heard the gold
coming up but us we keep
running around with band-aids we
can't understand how the judge
could be such an old fart we keep
scratching it we smear the spermy
gook on we kiss it we say there
there and everyone is laughing
and laughing the rich people
cracking pearls in their stomachs
the hungry people licking plain
stones they're hysterical they say
there there babies there there
there poor babies

Bad Mouth

FOR W. S. MERWIN

not bad mouth
in bad mouth
you know how to beat women so they love you afterwards
and come crawling
how to torture whole races and next time they fight
on the same side as you the lamb out of you
bad mouth lives in three houses with scabbards
bad mouth has hurt since the dinosaurs
even his sperm hurts
like napalm
bad mouth thinking
who do I kill?
who lock up in my arms for the last moment? pity
me pity me

good mouth I want to be vile enough for us both
so we'll love more
I want scorpion ladies I want beautiful pain ladies
and wolf brothers to lick their clear breasts with
good mouth worshipping
good mouth wreathing his genes like fuses
good mouth
I want being able to say help me
help me good mouth
the ones down to the raisin like my tongue
are my tongue the last ones before peace
are inside me
good mouth whoever I let live murdered me whoever I pitied burned
please stop me

This Day

probably death fits all right in the world
but every time somebody dies his mother
botches it suddenly she thinks there's not
enough room in her breasts the nipples
are clogged she says the ducts jammed rifles even
so old they sag like laundry she grabs
them and hangs on she doesn't understand she
says she can't understand it mother what
I'm doing is truth mother understand
me at least freedom but o god she can't find
space for an atom her glands burst her
pores swell like bad fruit mother when
we were wolves remember? she doesn't
understand the inside of bodies the voids
wasted the patient holes used up
like planets when I count three she says
everything was a dream everything before
now was really dead was I really dead?

The Long Bells

dream please
no favors
your last one
the wings closing the spirit lady the blue
was too much for me
I'd like not to know things like that anymore I'm
not superman it hurts me
I'd like to live in a cigarette advertisement
I'd like to just walk out
and beat my belly like a drum
until they scratched my name off
dream
I want to get dark like you
I want to live with the people named star who get worn down
to the moon by jump ropes and being unfolded
is there anything that would come through like a mountain
and look and go back and take that long I want that one
I have never said no more
dream
but I am now
no more please no more
I mean it

The Rabbit Fights for His Life
The Leopard Eats Lunch

FOR HARVEY FINKLE

what if the revolution comes and I'm in it and my job
is to murder a child accidentally
or afterwards to get rid of the policemen?
I had a milkshake last week with a policeman
we talked about his pay raise it eats shit
he told me what if I have that one? SAVAGE
the baby was easy
the baby went up in thin air
I remembered in dostoevsky where they talked
about whether it would all be worth the death of one child
and you decided yes or no according to your character
my character
is how he got back in his car
like a tired businessman and listened to the radio
for a few minutes
and waved
is having to lug him everywhere
I go because I can't take him to his wife crying like this
the children have learned to throw their arms around you
without meaning it to kiss you without feeling it
to know there is something marvelous
and not pay attention
in order to say any of this at all to you
I have made myself up like somebody
in a novel
in order not
to go out of my mind I make it I can only do two things
hold you
bury you

For Children When They Grow Up

god is simpler than you are
he's like the one carrying bricks
or you can make girls out of him there is a huge cunt it devours you
you lean back you say SAY SOMETHING
you say LOVE ME YOU ARE LIKE HITLER
YOU ARE A ZERO I CAN SEE THROUGH and you see through
the freezing bodies the mouths ashes
I don't remember what else

god I don't remember what else
it was about how easy it is an up and a down?
dying and being born backwards
and having to come in backwards?
god is like one wing he is one hand
I'm so lonely
god so
broken

Cracks

FOR GLORIA MILGROM

big mercy and little mercy big mercy
eats people they're like governments they can't sleep it cracks
them like toy cars they are this little they're on fire
so little mercy
spits the last drop on them they sizzle off like butter
you're big mercy I'm little it doesn't matter
I'm going to make love to you like a radio
I'm going to make things out of you and sell them back
to you so you'll be the same but some cheaper
then
little mercy says you look nice don't be sad
I'm big mercy now I drag by like a battle I want
not hitting you when you weren't kind I want if I loved you
saying is it different?
then truth comes for a long time
so you don't have to start anywhere people go in jail and then
    out people
hungry people in the crazy house big mercy
is in there his hand is named sparrow
she talks to his hand
in her lap
like a little dog it looks up
what about suicide in the red?
what about living in one valve and remembering?
little mercy lines up in its places you kiss them you
hold on so tight they start choking you can't stop they keep
    choking
on the other side
is who you would marry berserk
from gentleness
and in the house in the field in the last country
wild

Cellophane

if only we weren't so small next to the stars
we could refuse absolutely to be alive in this eon
to be alive now you can't understand one thing without pain
you can't feel your own face in the morning
without wanting to blow up
if we were bigger
we wouldn't keep happening over and over
like truth that hurts worse than anything
with NO big as the mint
and DO IT filling the air like soot from the incinerator
we'd be as easy as the game war
the wingspan from one death to another
and the centuries the unending centuries
taken away from us in cattle cars
would wail harmlessly
like ghosts

The Rampage

a baby got here once who before
he was all the way out and could already feel the hindu
pain inside him and the hebrew and the iliad
decided he was never going to stop crying no matter what
until they did something he wasn't going
to turn the horror
off in their fat sentences
and in the light bulb how much murder to get light
and in the walls agony agony for the bricks for the glaze
he was going to keep screaming
until they made death little like he was
and loved him too and sent
him back to undo all this
and it happened
he kept screaming he scared them he saw them
filling with womblight again like stadiums
he saw the tears sucked back into the story the smiles
opening like sandwiches
so he stopped
and looked up and said all right
it's better now
I'm hungry now I want just to sleep
and they let him

Inches

it would be wonderful to be quiet now
to creak down through the fossils making my last speech
into the blind rocks
or to hang from the bars by my belt
and not speak of us our bellows of helplessness our disgust
to be as silent as planets
even the wind has been burned out
hospitals jails the places learning to be hard like men
something where we would be taken and dispirited
of all things like god to godhead love
in peace
not to have "of" to our deaths anymore
the political would go into the back
it would bury itself in itself
and cry for us
I remember you you were my friend I loved you
very much of it was not for words

Crawl

the bottom of the universe and
cock-monster and piggy we
are crying for each other
we are stumbling out to go
work cock-monster the kiss so
everything but the skin melts
and you are sucked out piggy
flattening on the scum
like a rubber the girl
peeling an orange the doctor
dragging his shoelaces
like flesh cock-monster
in the eighth world I will kill
you with my vagina I
will roast you on the spit
of my forehead piggy
nothing's for sale is
it? except us? no more
flowers fruit the bitter
leaves underneath us we
are sown in the dark
back of death but even us
do you know really?

The Sting

the not want
jesus
I didn't know this the not want
for woman country daughter the man
hit rocked back crying holding him
the not want
for wounding myself for your mouth
for what my hand is opening getting sleepy
the not want
to ride hooked in you like a thistle
for long grass the earth broken to take breaths
in you
jesus
not want
for dreaming
to be president
to take the whole nation and kiss it
awake being born being desired
not new minds not even not
this grown into the big
and fuller
not want
for being able to not want
for trees taking me underneath clouds
taking me fury
exaltation
why? why baby? why dog? why wife?
why
not want president?
why not want friend with no anguish?
why
angel I love you god I love you why
not want heart in my body in each hand
picture guitar

holy
leave this
let this be here
let me
not want this not

The Last

when I was sleeping this morning one of my feet
fell out of the covers and my daughter
came in and covered it up with her little dolly blanket

I was dreaming right then that flames were shooting out of my
   cock
and when I woke up with her patting the soft cloth down on me
I believed I understood the end of eternity for the first time

don't ever make me explain this

In the Heart of the Beast

1

this is fresh meat right mr nixon?

this is even sweeter than mickey schwerner or fred hampton right?
even more tender than the cherokee nation or guatemala or greece
having their asses straightened for them isn't it?

this is none of your oriental imitation
this is iowa corn grown
this is jersey tomato grown
washington salmon maryland crab
this is from children
who'd barely begun ingesting corruption
the bodies floating belly up like polluted fish in cambodia
barely tainting them
the black kids blown up in their churches
hardly souring them
their torments were so meager
they still thought about life
still struggled with urgency
and compassion
so
tender

2

I'm sorry

I don't want to hear anymore that the innocent farmer in ohio on guard
    duty means well but is fucked up by his politicians and raises his rifle

out of some primal fear for his own life and his family's and that he
hates niggers hates them hates them because he is warped and deceived
by events

and pulls the trigger

I'm sorry I don't want to forgive him anymore
I don't want to say he didn't know what he was doing
because he knew what he was doing
because he didn't pull the trigger once and run away screaming
they kept shooting the kids said
we thought they were blanks but they kept shooting and shooting
we were so scared

I don't want to forgive the bricklayer from akron who might or might
    not hate his mother I don't care or the lawyer or gas station attendant
    from cleveland who may or may not have had a bad childhood
I don't care
I don't want to know
I don't want to hear anything about it

another kid said the rocks weren't even reaching them!

I don't want to understand why they did it

how could you?
just that

everything else is pure shit

3

on the front page of the times a girl is screaming
she will be screaming forever
and her friend will lie there forever you wouldn't know she
    wasn't just sleeping in the sun except for the other screaming

and on the editorial page
"the tragic nature of the division of the country . . . the provocation
    undoubtedly was great and was also unpardonable . . ."

o my god
my god

if there was a way to purify the world who would be left?
there is a list
and it says
this person for doing this
and that person for doing nothing
and this person for not howling in rage
and that for desperately hanging on to the reasons the reasons
and
there is an avenger
who would be left?
who is there now who isn't completely insane from all this?
who didn't dream with me last night
of burning everything destroying everyone
of tearing pieces of your own body off
of coughing your language up and spitting it away like vomit
of wanting to start at the bottom of your house
breaking everything floor by floor
burning the pictures
tearing the mattresses up
smashing windows and chairs until nothing is left
and then the cars with a sledgehammer
the markets
the stores that sell things
the buses
the bridges into the city
the airports
the international harbors
the tall buildings crumpling like corpses
the theaters torn down to the bare stage
the galleries naked the bookstores like mouths open

there should be funerals in front of the white house
bones in the capitol

where do you stop?

how can we be like this?

4

I remember what it was to come downstairs
and my daughter would be there crawling toward me as fast as she
 could
crying HI DADDA HI DADDA

and what it was to bury my face in my wife's breasts and forget

to touch a friend's shoulder
to laugh
to take walks

5

I don't want to call anyone pig

meeting people who tell you they want war they hate communists
or somebody who'll say they hate niggers spics kikes
and you still don't believe they're beyond knowing
because you feel comfortable with them even drawn to them
and know somehow that they have salvageable hearts
you try to keep hope
for a community that could contain both of you
so that you'd both be generous and loving
and find ways that didn't need hatred and killing
to burn off the inarticulate human rage at having to die

I thought if I could take somebody like that in my arms
I could convince them that everyone was alone before death
but love saved us from living our lives reflexively with death

that it could happen
we would be naked now
we'd change now little by little
we'd be better
we would just be here
in this life

but it could be a delusion couldn't it?
it could be like thinking those soldiers were shooting blanks
up until the last second standing there scared shitless
but inside
thinking americans don't shoot innocent people!
I know it!
I learned it in school in the movies!
it doesn't happen like this
and hearing a bullet slam into the ground next to you and the flesh
and every voice in your body saying o no no
and seeing your friend go down
half her head blown away
and the image of kennedy in back of the car
and of king
and the other kennedy
and wanting to explode o no no no no no

6

not to be loaded up under the flopping bladewash the tubes sucking to
    be thrown out turning to flame burning on trees on grass on skin
    burning lips away breasts away genitals arms legs buttocks
not to be torn out of the pack jammed in the chamber belched out laid
    over the ground like a live fence of despair
not to fog down into the river where the fish die into the rice where the
    frogs die into the trees where the fruit dies the grain dies the leaves
    into the genes

into the generations

more black children
more red children
and yellow

not to be screaming

The Lark.
The Thrush.
The Starling.
(Poems from
Issa)

In the next life,
butterfly,
a thousand years from now,

we'll sit like this
again
under the tree

in the dust,
hearing it, this
great thing.

•

I sit in my room.

Outside, haze.

The whole world
is haze

and I can't figure out
one room.

•

So
mucked up with
kneading
dough she is

she has to use
her wrist to
push her hair back
from her eyes.

•

That the world
is going
to end someday
does not concern
the wren:

it's time to
build your nest,
you build
your nest.

.

Spring: another
joke.

This run-down
house: me.

Go ahead, ask,
how's
spring?

Average, just
average.

.

You're two, that's great.
Go ahead, laugh, crawl
around.

You'll find
out,
you'll see.

.

Winter,
damn,
again.

Same
frost, same
fire.

•

Listen carefully.

I'm meditating.
The only thing in my mind
right now
is the wind.

No, wait . . . the autumn
wind, that's right,
the *autumn* wind!

•

The hail goes
dancing
into the fire.
The coal flares.

I watch the embers
going out, one
by
one.

•

What a sound his
shell made, that
big cockroach! *Crack!*
like a churchbell:
Crack!
Crack!
Crack!

•

They wash you
when
you're born, then,
when you're finished,
if you're very lucky,
you get washed
again.

·

A holiday:
every
yard or
two, in
the grass,
among
the flowers,
along
the rushing
stream,
picnickers are
sprawled.

·

What we are
given:
resignation.

What is
taken from us:
resignation.

It is ours that
we can see, do
see, must see

our own bones
bleaching
under the warm moon.

·

Baby, I don't want
to tell you
again: you can't go out
in weather like this.

Can't you teach
yourself to play
checkers or
something?

•

The most excruciating
thing
I could imagine: to see,
the way
I am now,

the place where I
was born
with all its
mist
blown away.

•

In the middle
of a bite of
grass,
the turtle stops
to listen for,
oh, an
hour, two
hours,
three hours . . .

•

When
you were small, I
put you
in
a swing, you
held
a flower.

Next thing
I
knew . . .

•

This is what,
at last, it is
to be
a human being.

Leaving nothing
out, not
one star, one
wren, one tear
out.

•

I'd forgotten and
how could I ever
have
my mother, peeling
the apple, giving me
the heart-
flesh.

•

That night,
winter,
rain,
the mountains.

No guilt. No
not-guilt.
Winter,
rain,
mountains.

.

I know
nothing anymore
of roads.

Winter
is a road,
I know,

but the body,
the beloved
body,

is it, too,
only a kind
of road?

.

The fleas, too,
have fled
my burned-down
house. Oh,

there you are,
old friend, and
oh, you, too,
old,
old friend.

.

It's over now. I watch
the fire. I watch the firelight
wash
the wall. I watch
the shadow on
it of the woman.

I don't
understand it, but
I watch, I
watch.

•

Did I write this
as I was
dying?

Did I really
write
this?

That I wanted to thank
the snow
fallen on my blanket?

Could I
have written
this?

With

Ignorance

The Sanctity

FOR NICK AND ARLENE DE CREDICO

The men working on the building going up here have got these great,
little motorized wheelbarrows that're supposed to be for lugging bricks
  and mortar
but that they seem to spend most of their time barrel-assing up the street
  in,
racing each other or trying to con the local secretaries into taking rides
  in the bucket.
I used to work on jobs like that and now when I pass by the skeleton
  of the girders
and the tangled heaps of translucent brick wrappings, I remember the
  guys I was with then
and how hard they were to know. Some of them would be so good to
  be with at work,
slamming things around, playing practical jokes, laughing all the time,
  but they could be miserable,
touchy and sullen, always ready to imagine an insult or get into a fight
  anywhere else.
If something went wrong, if a compressor blew or a truck backed over
  somebody,
they'd be the first ones to risk their lives dragging you out
but later you'd see them and they'd be drunk, looking for trouble, almost
  murderous,
and it would be frightening trying to figure out which person they really
  were.
Once I went home to dinner with a carpenter who'd taken me under
  his wing
and was keeping everyone off my back while he helped me. He was
  beautiful but at his house, he sulked.
After dinner, he and the kids and I were watching television while his
  wife washed the dishes
and his mother, who lived with them, sat at the table holding a big
  cantaloupe in her lap,

fondling it and staring at it with the kind of intensity people usually
only look into fires with.
The wife kept trying to take it away from her but the old lady squawked
and my friend said, "Leave her alone, will you?" "But she's doing it on
purpose," the wife said.
I was watching. The mother put both her hands on it then, with her
thumbs spread,
as though the melon were a head and her thumbs were covering the eyes
and she was aiming it like a gun or a camera.
Suddenly the wife muttered, "You bitch!" ran over to the bookshelf,
took a book down—
A *History of Revolutions*—rattled through the pages and triumphantly
handed it to her husband.
A photograph: someone who's been garroted and the executioner, stand-
ing behind him in a business hat,
has his thumbs just like that over the person's eyes, straightening the
head,
so that you thought the thumbs were going to move away because they
were only pointing
the person at something they wanted him to see and the one with the
hands was going to say, "Look! Right there!"
"I told you," the wife said. "I swear to god she's trying to drive me
crazy."
I didn't know what it all meant but my friend went wild, started breaking
things, I went home
and when I saw him the next morning at breakfast he acted as though
nothing had happened.
We used to eat at the Westfield truck stop, but I remember Fritz's, The
Victory, The Eagle,
and I think I've never had as much contentment as I did then, before
work, the light just up,
everyone sipping their coffee out of the heavy white cups and teasing
the middle-aged waitresses
who always acted vaguely in love with whoever was on jobs around
there right then
besides the regular farmers on their way back from the markets and the
long-haul truckers.

Listen: sometimes when you go to speak about life it's as though your
        mouth's full of nails
but other times it's so easy that it's ridiculous to even bother.
The eggs and the toast could fly out of the plates and it wouldn't matter
and the bubbles in the level could blow sky-high and it still wouldn't.
Listen to the back-hoes gearing up and the shouts and somebody cracking
        his sledge into the mortar pan.
Listen again. He'll do it all day if you want him to. Listen again.

Spit

*. . . then the son of the "superior race" began to spit into the Rabbi's mouth
so that the Rabbi could continue to spit on the Torah . . .*
—THE BLACK BOOK

After this much time, it's still impossible. The SS man with his stiff hair
        and his uniform;
the Rabbi, probably in a torn overcoat, probably with a stained beard
        the other would be clutching;
the Torah, God's word, on the altar, the letters blurring under the
        blended phlegm;
the Rabbi's parched mouth, the SS man perfectly absorbed, obsessed
        with perfect humiliation.
So many years and what is there to say still about the soldiers waiting
        impatiently in the snow,
about the one stamping his feet, thinking, Kill him! Get it over with!
while back there the lips of the Rabbi and the other would have brushed
and if time had stopped you would have thought they were lovers,
so lightly kissing, the sharp, luger hand under the dear chin,
the eyes furled slightly and then when it started again the eyelashes of
        both of them
shyly fluttering as wonderfully as the pulse of a baby.
Maybe we don't have to speak of it at all, it's still the same.
War, that happens and stops happening but is always somehow right
        there, twisting and hardening us;
then what we make of God—words, spit, degradation, murder, shame;
        every conceivable torment.
All these ways to live that have something to do with how we live
and that we're almost ashamed to use as metaphors for what goes on
        in us
but that we do anyway, so that love is battle and we watch ourselves
        in love
become maddened with pride and incompletion, and God is what it is
        when we're alone
wrestling with solitude and everything speaking in our souls turns against
        us like His fury

and just facing another person, there is so much terror and hatred that
        yes,
spitting in someone's mouth, trying to make him defile his own meaning,
would signify the struggle to survive each other and what we'll enact to
        accomplish it.

There's another legend.
It's about Moses, that when they first brought him as a child before
        Pharaoh,
the king tested him by putting a diamond and a live coal in front of him
and Moses picked up the red ember and popped it into his mouth
so for the rest of his life he was tongue-tied and Aaron had to speak for
        him.
What must his scarred tongue have felt like in his mouth?
It must have been like always carrying something there that weighed
        too much,
something leathery and dead whose greatest gravity was to loll out like
        an ox's,
and when it moved, it must have been like a thick embryo slowly coming
        alive,
butting itself against the inner sides of his teeth and cheeks.
And when God burned in the bush, how could he not cleave to him?
How could he not know that all of us were on fire and that every word
        we said would burn forever,
in pain, unquenchably, and that God knew it, too, and would say nothing
        Himself ever again beyond this,
ever, but would only live in the flesh that we use like firewood,
in all the caves of the body, the gut cave, the speech cave:
He would slobber and howl like something just barely a man that beats
        itself again and again onto the dark,
moist walls away from the light, away from whatever would be light
        for this last eternity.
"Now therefore go," He said, "and I will be with thy mouth."

Toil

After the argument—argument? battle, war, harrowing; you need
    shrieks, moans from the pit—
after that woman and I anyway stop raking each other with the meat-
    hooks we've become with each other,
I fit my forehead into the smudge I've already sweated onto the window
    with a thousand other exhaustions
and watch an old man having breakfast out of a pile of bags on my
    front step.
Peas from a can, bread with the day-old price scrawled over the label
    in big letters
and then a bottle that looks so delectable, the way he carefully unsheathes
    it
so the neck just lips out of the wrinkled foreskin of the paper and closes
    his eyes and tilts,
long and hard, that if there were one lie left in me to forgive a last
    rapture of cowardice
I'd go down there too and sprawl and let the whole miserable rest go
    to pieces.
Does anyone still want to hear how love can turn rotten?
How you can be so desperate that even going adrift wouldn't be
    enough—
you want to scour yourself out, get rid of all the needs you've still got
    in yourself
that keep you endlessly tearing against yourself in rages of guilt and
    frustration?
I don't. I'd rather think about other things. Beauty. How do you learn
    to believe there's beauty?
The kids going by on their way to school with their fat little lunch bags:
    beauty!
My old drunk with his bags—bottle bags, rag bags, shoe bags: beauty!
    beauty!
He lies there like the goddess of wombs and first-fruit, asleep in the
    riches,
one hand still hooked in mid-flight over the intricacies of the iron railing.

Old father, wouldn't it be a good ending if you and I could just walk
    away together?
Or that you were the king who reveals himself, who folds back the
    barbed, secret wings
and we're all so in love now, one spirit, one flesh, one generation, that
    the truces don't matter?
Or maybe a better ending would be that there is no ending.
Maybe the Master of Endings is wandering down through his herds to
    find it
and the cave cow who tells truth and the death cow who holds sea in
    her eyes are still there
but all he hears are the same old irresistible slaughter-pen bawlings.
So maybe there is no end to the story and maybe there's no story.
Maybe the last calf just ambles up to the trough through the clearing
and nudges aside the things that swarm on the water and her mouth
    dips in among them and drinks.
Then she lifts, and it pours, everything, gushes, and we're lost in both
    waters.

The Last Deaths

1

A few nights ago I was half-watching the news on television and half-
    reading to my daughter.
The book was about a boy who makes a zoo out of junk he finds in a
    lot—
I forget exactly; a horse-bottle, a bedspring that's a snake, things like
    that—
and on the news they were showing a film about the most recent
    bombings.
There was a woman crying, tearing at her hair and breasts, shrieking
    incomprehensibly
because her husband and all her children had been killed the night before
and just when she'd flung herself against the legs of one of the soldiers
    watching her,
Jessie looked up and said, "What's the matter with her? Why's she
    crying?"

2

I haven't lived with my daughter for a year now and sometimes it still
    hurts not to be with her more,
not to have her laughter when I want it or to be able to comfort her
    when she cries out in her sleep.
I don't see her often enough to be able to know what I can say to her,
what I can solve for her without introducing more confusions than there
    were in the first place.
That's what happened with death. She was going to step on a bug and
    when I told her she'd kill it,
it turned out that no one had ever told her about death and now she
    had to know.
"It's when you don't do anything anymore," I told her. "It's like being
    asleep."
I didn't say for how long but she's still been obsessed with it since then,

wanting to know if she's going to die and when and if I am and her
mother and grandma and do robbers do it?
Maybe I should have just given her the truth, but I didn't: now what
was I going to say about that woman?
"Her house fell down," I said. "Who knocked down her house?" "It
just fell."
Then I found something for us to do, but last night, again, first thing,
"Tell me about that girl." "What girl?" "You know." Of course I know.
What could have gone on in my child's dreams last night so that woman
was a girl now?
How many times must they have traded places back and forth in that
innocent crib?
"You mean the lady whose house fell down?" "Yeah, who knocked her
house down?"

3

These times. The endless wars. The hatreds. The vengefulness.
Everyone I know getting out of their marriage. Old friends distrustful.
The politicians using us until you can't think about it anymore because
you can't tell anymore
which reality affects which and how do you escape from it without
everything battering you back again?
How many times will I lie to Jessie about things that have no meaning
for either of us?
How many forgivenesses will I need from her when all I wanted was to
keep her from suffering the same ridiculous illusions I have?
There'll be peace soon.
They'll fling it down like sick meat we're supposed to lick up and be
thankful for and what then?

4

Jessie, it's as though the whole race is sunk in an atmosphere of blood
and it's been clotting for so many centuries we can hardly move now.
Someday, you and I will face each other and turn away and the absence,
the dread, will flame between us like an enormous, palpable word that
wasn't spoken.

Do we only love because we're weak and murderous?
Are we commended to each other to alleviate our terror of solitude and
annihilation and that's all?

5

I wish I could change dreams with you, baby. I've had the bad ones,
what comes now is calm and abstract.
Last night, while you and that poor woman were trading deaths like
horrible toys,
I was dreaming about the universe. The whole universe was happening
in one day, like a blossom,
and during that day people's voices kept going out to it, crying, "Stop!
Stop!"
The universe didn't mind, though. It knew we were only cursing love
again
because we didn't know how to love, not even for a day,
but our little love days were just seeds it blew out on parachutes into
the summer wind.
Then you and I were there. We shouted "Stop!" too. We kept wanting
the universe to explode,
we kept wishing it would go back into its root, but the universe
understood.
We were its children. It let us cry into its petals, it let its stems bend
against us,
then it fed and covered us and we looked up sleepily—it was time to
sleep—
and whatever our lives were, our love, this once, was enough.

The Race of the Flood

The way someone stays home, that's all, stays in the house, in the room,
     just stays,
the way she, let it be she this time, the way she stays, through the class,
     the backseat and the job;
the way she stays there for so many chapters, so many reels, not moving,
     the way the earth doesn't move;
the way one morning, one day, any day, she wakes and knows now that
     it's gone now,
that never is now, and she thinks she can feel it, the never, even her cells
     have spread over the sheets;
the way she thinks that oh, even these open-pored pores, even these
     glances butting the wall like thrown-away combs;
the way she, or these, these pores, glances, presences, so me, so within
     me,
as though I were she, exactly, as though I were the absence, too, the
     loss, too,
as though just beneath me was the worn, soft tallow, the unmoved and
     unmoving;
so there is this within me which has never touched life, never, never
     gone to the ball or the war,
never and never, so within and next and around me, fear and fear and
     the self-deceived,
the turned-to-the-wall, the stricken, untouched, begun ill or never begun,
the way it happens without happening, begins or doesn't, moves, gives
     way, or never does.

Or this. Messages, codes; the way he, the next one, the way he pins
     them all over himself,
on his clothes, on his skin, and then walks through the street like a
     signpost, a billboard;
the way there are words to his wife and words to his kids, words even
     to god so our lord
is over his eyes and our father over his belly and the history of madness
     and history of cliffs;

the way there's no room now, the way every word in the world has
   stuck to the skin
and is used up now, and his eyes move, roll, spin up to the top of his
   head
the way the eyes of those fish who try to see god or the lid of the water
   roll, like dice,
so me, within me again: I cover myself with my own scrawl and wait
   in the shallow,
I face the shallow and wait like a fin and I ripple the membrane of scrawl
   like water;
so me, we, dear life I love you where are you, so we, dear our lord of
   anguish where are you,
so zero, so void; we don't even know how to end it, how to get out of
   the way of the serif or slash.

And the next, and the next, the way the next, the way all, any, any he,
   any she,
any human or less or more, if not bone that leaps with its own word
   then still more,
if not skin that washes its own wound then more and more, the way
   more than a wound,
more than a thing which has to be spoken or born, born now, later,
   again,
the way desire is born and born, the desire within me and not, within
   and without and neither;
the way the next holds on to itself and the one after holds on to me, on
   to my person, my human,
and I give back, the way ten times a day I offer it back with love or
   resentment or horror,
so I bear my likeness and greet my like, and the way will, my will or
   not,
the way all it can say is I am or am not, or I don't, won't, cannot or
   will not,
and the way that it burns anyway, and the way it smiles, smiles anyway,
   fills, ripens,
so that the hour or the scrawl burns and ripens; so within me, as though
   I had risen,

146

as though I had gone to the gate and opened the lock and stepped
through;
so within me, it lifts and goes through, lifts itself through, and burns,
anyway, smiles, anyway.

Bob

If you put in enough hours in bars, sooner or later you get to hear every
    imaginable kind of bullshit.

Every long-time loser has a history to convince you he isn't living at the
    end of his own leash

and every kid has some pimple on his psyche he's trying to compensate
    for with an epic,

but the person with the most unlikely line I'd ever heard—he told me
    he'd killed, more than a few times,

during the war and then afterwards working for the mob in Philadel-
    phia—I could never make up my mind about.

He was big, bigger than big. He'd also been drinking hard and wanted
    to be everyone's friend

and until the bartender called the cops because he wouldn't stop stuffing
    money in girls' blouses,

he gave me his life: the farm childhood, the army, re-upping, the war—
    that killing—

coming back and the new job—that killing—then almost being killed
    himself by another hood and a kind of pension,

a distributorship, incredibly enough, for hairdresser supplies in the ward
    around Passyunk and Mifflin.

He left before the cops came, and before he left he shook my hand and
    looked into my eyes.

It's impossible to tell how much that glance weighed: it was like having
    to lift something,

something so ponderous and unwieldy that you wanted to call for some-
    one to help you

and when he finally turned away, it wouldn't have bothered me at all
    if I'd never seen him again.

This is going to get a little nutty now, maybe because everything was a
    little nutty for me back then.

Not a little. I'd been doing some nice refining. No work, no woman,
    hardly any friends left.

The details don't matter. I was helpless, self-pitying, angry, inert, and
    right now
I was flying to Detroit to interview for a job I knew I wouldn't get.
    Outside,
the clouds were packed against our windows and just as I let my book
    drop to look out,
we broke through into a sky so brilliant that I had to close my eyes
    against the glare.
I stayed like that, waiting for the stinging after-light to fade, but it seemed
    to pulse instead,
then suddenly it washed strangely through me, swelling, powdering,
and when my sight came back, I was facing inwards, into the very center
    of myself,
a dark, craggy place, and there was a sound that when I blocked the
    jets,
the hiss of the pressurization valves and the rattling silverware and
    glasses, I realized was laughter.
The way I was then, I think nothing could have shocked me. I was a
    well, I'd fallen in,
someone was there with me, but all I did was drift until I came to him:
    a figure, arms lifted,
he was moving in a great, cumbersome dance, full of patience, full of
    time, and that laughter,
a deep, flowing tumult of what seemed to be songs from someone else's
    life.
Now the strange part. My ears were ringing, my body felt like water,
    but I moved again,
farther in, until I saw the face of who it was with me and it was Bob,
    the drunk,
or if it wasn't him, his image filled the space, the blank, the template,
    better than anyone else,
and so, however doubtful it seems now, I let it be him: he was there, I
    let him stay.
Understand, this happened quickly. By that night, home again, I was
    broken again,
torn, crushed on the empty halves of my bed, but for that time, from
    Pittsburgh, say,

until we braked down to the terminal in Detroit, I smiled at that self in
    myself,
his heavy dance, his laughter winding through the wrack and detritus
    of what I thought I was.

Bob, I don't know what happened to. He probably still makes the circuits
    of the clubs and corner bars,
and there must be times when strangers listen and he can tell it, the
    truth or his nightmare of it.
"I killed people," the secret heart opening again, "and Jesus God, I
    didn't even know them."

Bread

A whole section of the city I live in has been urban renewed, some of
     it torn down,
some restored to what it was supposed to have been a few hundred
     years ago.
Once you could've walked blocks without hearing English, now the
     ghettos have been cleared,
there are parks and walkways and the houses are all owned by people
     who've moved back from the suburbs.
When I lived there, at the very edge of it where the expressway is going
     in now
and the buildings are still boarded with plywood or flattened altogether,
the old market was already shuttered, the shipping depots had been
     relocated upriver
and the only person I ever saw was a grocer who lived across from me
     over his empty store.
I couldn't understand what he was doing there—it must have been years
since a customer had come in past the dead register and the icebox
     propped open with a carton,
but it was comforting to have him: he'd make his bed, sweep, cook for
     himself like a little wife
and when the constables came every week or so to tell us we were
     condemned,
he never paid attention so I didn't either. I didn't want to leave. I'd been
     in love,
I thought I was healing, for all I know I might have stayed forever in
     the grim room I was camped in
but one day some boys who must have climbed up through one of the
     abandoned tenements
suddenly appeared skidding and wrestling over the steep pitch of the
     old man's roof
and when I shouted at them to get the hell off, he must have thought
     I'd meant him:
he lurched in his bed and stopped rubbing himself with the white cream
     he used to use on his breasts.

He looked up, our eyes met, and I think for the first time he really
      believed I was there.
I don't know how long we stared at each other—I could hear the kids
      shrieking at me
and the road-building equipment that had just started tearing the skin
      from the avenue—
then his zincy fingers slowly subsided against his heart and he smiled,
a brilliant, total, incongruous smile, and even though I had no desire to,
the way afterwards I had no desire to cry when my children were born,
      but did,
sobbed, broke down with joy or some inadmissible apprehension, I
      smiled back.
It was as though we were lovers, as though, like lovers, we'd made
      speech again
and were listening as it gutted and fixed the space between us and then
      a violent,
almost physical loathing took me, for all I'd done to have ended in this
      place,
to myself, to everyone, to the whole business we're given the name life
      for.

I could go on with this. I could call it a victory, an exemplary triumph,
      but I'd lie.
Sometimes the universe inside us can assume the aspect of places we've
      been
so that instead of emotions we see trees we knew or touched or a path,
and instead of the face of a thought, there'll be an unmade bed, a car
      nosing from an alley.
All I know about that time is that it stayed, that something, pain or the
      fear of it,
makes me stop the wheel and reach to the silence beyond my eyes and
      it's still there:
the empty wind, the white crosses of the renewers slashed on the
      doorposts,
the last, dim layers of paint loosening from the rotted sills, drifting
      downwards.

Near the Haunted Castle

Teen Gangs Fight: Girl Paralyzed By Police Bullet
—HEADLINE

This is a story. You don't have to think about it, it's make-believe.
It's like a lie, maybe not quite a lie but I don't want you to worry about
      it.
The reason it's got to be a lie is because you already know the truth
      and I already know it
and what difference does it make? We still can't do anything: why kill
      yourself?
So here's the story. It's like the princess and the pea, remember?
Where they test her with mattresses and a pea and she's supposed not
      to sleep
and get upset and then they'll know she's the princess and marry her?
Except in this version, she comes in and nobody believes it's her and
      they lay her down
but instead of forty mattresses do you know what they lay her on?
      Money!
Of course, money! A million dollars! It's like a hundred mattresses, it's
      so soft, a thousand!
It's how much you cut from the budget for teachers to give the policemen.
It's how much you take from relief to trade for bullets. Soft!
And instead of the pea, what? A bullet! Brilliant! A tiny bullet stuck in
      at the bottom!
So then comes the prince. My prince, my beauty. Except he has holsters.
He has leather and badges. And what he does, he starts tearing the
      mattresses out.
Out? Don't forget, it's a story. Don't forget to not worry, it's pretend.
He's tearing the mattresses out and then he's stuffing them in his mouth!
This wonderful prince-mouth, this story-mouth, it holds millions,
      billions,
and she's falling, slowly, or no, the pea, the bullet, is rising,
surging like some ridiculous funny snout out of the dark down there.
Does it touch you? Oh, yes, but don't worry, this is just a fib, right?

It slides next to your skin and it's cold and it goes in, in! as though you
        were a door,
as though you were the whole bedroom; in, through the backbone,
        through the cartilage,
the cords, then it freezes. It freezes and the prince is all gone,
this is the sleeping, the wrong-sleeping, you shouldn't be sleeping,
the so-heaviness in the arms, the so-heaviness in the legs, don't sleep,
        they'll leave you,
they'll throw you away . . . the dollars spinning, the prince leaving,
and you, at the bottom, on the no-turning, on the pea, like a story,
on the bullet, the single bullet that costs next to nothing, like one dollar.
People torture each other so they'll tell the whole truth, right?
And study the nervous systems of the lower orders to find the truth,
        right?
And tell the most obviously absurd tales for the one grain of truth?
The mother puts down her book and falls asleep watching television.
On the television they go on talking.
The father's in bed, the little gears still rip through his muscles.
The two brothers have the same dream, like Blinken and Nod, like the
        mayor and the president.
The sister . . . The sister . . . The heart furnace, the brain furnace, hot
        . . . hot . . .
Let's go back to find where the truth is. Let's find the beginning.
In the beginning was love, right? No, in the beginning . . . the
        bullet . . .

The Cave

I think most people are relieved the first time they actually know someone
who goes crazy.

It doesn't happen the way you hear about it where the person gibbers
and sticks to you like an insect:

mostly there's crying, a lot of silence, sometimes someone will whisper
back to their voices.

All my friend did was sit, at home until they found him, then for hours
at a time on his bed in the ward,

pointing at his eyes, chanting the same phrase over and over. "Too much
fire!" he'd say. "Too much fire!"

I remember I was amazed at how raggedy he looked, then annoyed
because he wouldn't answer me

and then, when he was getting better, I used to pester him to tell me
about that fire-thing.

He'd seemed to be saying he'd seen too much and I wanted to know
too much what

because my obsession then was that I was somehow missing everything
beyond the ordinary.

What was only real was wrong. There were secrets that could turn you
into stone,

they were out of range or being kept from me, but my friend, if he knew
what I meant, wouldn't say,

so we'd talk politics or books or moon over a beautiful girl who was
usually in the visiting room when we were

who mutilated herself. Every time I was there, new slashes would've
opened out over her forearms and wrists

and once there were two brilliant medallions on her cheeks that I thought
were rouge spots

but that my friend told me were scratches she'd put there with a broken
light bulb when she'd run away the day before.

The way you say running away in hospitals is "eloping." Someone who
hurts themself is a "cutter."

How could she do it to herself? My friend didn't think that was the
question.

She'd eloped, cut, they'd brought her back and now she was waiting
    there again,
those clowny stigmata of lord knows what on her, as tranquil and
    seductive as ever.
I used to storm when I'd leave her there with him. She looked so
    vulnerable.
All the hours they'd have. I tormented myself imagining how they'd
    come together,
how they'd tell each other the truths I thought I had to understand to
    live,
then how they'd kiss, their lips, chaste and reverent, rushing over the
    forgiven surfaces.
Tonight, how long afterwards, watching my wife undress, letting my
    gaze go so everything blurs
but the smudges of her nipples and hair and the wonderful lumpy graces
    of her pregnancy,
I still can bring it back: those dismal corridors, the furtive nods, the
    moans I thought were sexual
and the awful lapses that seemed vestiges of exaltations I would never
    have,
but now I know whatever in the mystery I was looking for, whatever
    brute or cloud I thought eluded me,
isn't lost in the frenzy of one soul or another, but next to us, in the
    touch, between.
Lying down, fumbling for the light, moving into the shadow with my
    son or daughter, I find it again:
the prism of hidden sorrow, the namelessness of nothing and nothing
    shuddering across me,
and then the warmth, clinging and brightening, the hide, the caul, the
    first mind.

Hog Heaven

FOR JAMES HAVARD

It stinks. It stinks and it stinks and it stinks and it stinks.
It stinks in the mansions and it stinks in the shacks and the carpeted offices,
in the beds and the classrooms and out in the fields where there's no one.
It just stinks. Sniff and feel it come up: it's like death coming up.
Take one foot, ignore it long enough, leave it on the ground long enough
because you're afraid to stop, even to love, even to be loved,
it'll stink worse than you can imagine, as though the whole air was meat pressing your eyelids,
as though you'd been caught, hung up from the earth
and all the stinks of the fear drain down and your toes are the valves dripping
the giant stinks of the pain and the death and the radiance.
Old people stink, with their teeth and their hot rooms, and the kiss,
the age-kiss, the death-kiss, it comes like a wave and you want to fall down and be over.
And money stinks: the little threads that go through it like veins through an eye,
each stinks—if you hold it onto your lip it goes bad, it stinks like a vein going bad.
And Christ stank: he knew how the slaves would be stacked into the holds and he took it—
the stink of the vomit and shit and of somebody just rolling over and plunging in with his miserable seed.
And the seed stinks. And the fish carrying it upstream and the bird eating the fish
and you the bird's egg, the dribbles of yolk, the cycle: the whole thing stinks.
The intellect stinks and the moral faculty, like things burning, like the cave under justice,
and the good quiet men, like oceans of tears squeezed into one handful, they stink,

and the whole consciousness, like something plugged up, stinks, like
    something cut off.
Life stinks and death stinks and god and your hand touching your face
and every breath, daring to turn, daring to come back from the stop:
    the turn stinks
and the last breath, the real one, the one where everyone troops into
    your bed
and piles on—oh, that one stinks best! It stays on your mouth
and who you kiss now knows life and knows death, knows how it would
    be to fume in a nostril
and the thousand desires that stink like the stars and the voice heard
    through the stars
and each time—milk sour, egg sour, sperm sour—each time—dirt,
    friend, father—
each time—mother, tree, breath—each time—breath and breath and
    breath—
each time the same stink, the amazement, the wonder to do this and it
    flares,
this, and it stinks, this: it stinks and it stinks and it stinks and it stinks.

Blades

When I was about eight, I once stabbed somebody, another kid, a little
    girl.
I'd been hanging around in front of the supermarket near our house
and when she walked by, I let her have it, right in the gap between her
    shirt and her shorts
with a piece of broken-off car antenna I used to carry around in my
    pocket.
It happened so fast I still don't know how I did it: I was as shocked as
    she was
except she squealed and started yelling as though I'd plunged a knife in
    her
and everybody in the neighborhood gathered around us, then they called
    the cops,
then the girl's mother came running out of the store saying "What
    happened? What happened?"
and the girl screamed, "He stabbed me!" and I screamed back, "I did
    not!" and she you did too
and me I didn't and we were both crying hysterically by that time.
Somebody pulled her shirt up and it was just a scratch but we went on
    and on
and the mother, standing between us, seemed to be absolutely terrified.
I still remember how she watched first one of us and then the other with
    a look of complete horror—
You did too! I did not!—as though we were both strangers, as though
    it was some natural disaster
she was beholding that was beyond any mode of comprehension so all
    she could do
was stare speechlessly at us, and then another expression came over her
    face,
one that I'd never seen before, that made me think she was going to cry
    herself
and sweep both of us, the girl and me, into her arms to hold us against
    her.
The police came just then, though, quieted everyone down, put the girl
    and the mother

into a squad-car to take to the hospital and me in another to take to
	jail
except they really only took me around the corner and let me go because
	the mother and daughter were black
and in those days you had to do something pretty terrible to get into
	trouble that way.

I don't understand how we twist these things or how we get them straight
	again
but I relived that day I don't know how many times before I realized I
	had it all wrong.
The boy wasn't me at all, he was another kid: I was just there.
And it wasn't the girl who was black, but him. The mother was real,
	though.
I really had thought she was going to embrace them both
and I had dreams about her for years afterwards: that I'd be being born
	again
and she'd be lifting me with that same wounded sorrow or she would
	suddenly appear out of nowhere,
blotting out everything but a single, blazing wing of holiness.
Who knows the rest? I can still remember how it felt the old way.
How I make my little thrust, how she crushes us against her, how I turn
	and snarl
at the cold circle of faces around us because something's torn in me,
some ancient cloak of terror we keep on ourselves because we'll do
	anything,
anything, not to know how silently we knell in the mouth of death
and not to obliterate the forgiveness and the lies we offer one another
	and call innocence.
This is innocence. I touch her, we kiss.
And this. I'm here or not here. I can't tell. I stab her. I stab her again.
	I still can't.

Friends

My friend Dave knew a famous writer who used to have screwdrivers
    for breakfast.
He'd start with half gin and half juice and the rest of the day he'd sit
    with the same glass
in the same chair and add gin. The drink would get paler and paler,
    finally he'd pass out.
Every day was the same. Sometimes, when I'm making milk for the baby,
    cutting the thick,
sweet formula from the can with sterilized water, the baby, hungry again,
    still hungry,
rattling his rickety, long-legged chair with impatience, I think of that
    story.
Dave says the writer could talk like a god. He'd go on for hours in the
    same thought.
In his books, though, you never find out why he drove so hard toward
    his death.
I have a death in my memory that lately the word itself always brings
    back. I'm not quite sure why.
A butterfly, during a downpour one afternoon, hooked onto my screen.
    I thought it was waiting.
The light was just so. Its eyes caught the flare so it seemed to be watching
    me in my bed.
When I got up to come closer and it should have been frightened, it
    hung on.
After the rain, it was still there. Its eyes were still shining. I touched the
    screen
and it fell to the ledge. There were blue streaks on its wings. A while
    later, the wind took it.
The writer drowned in his puke or his liver exploded—it depends on
    the story.
He was a strong man, for all that. He must have thought it was taking
    forever.
Dave says when he'd wake with amnesia, he wouldn't want you to fill
    in the gaps.

He just wanted his gin and his juice. From all that you hear, he was
   probably right.
When we were young and we'd drink our minds to extinction, that was
   the best part: you did this, you said that.
It was like hearing yourself in a story. Sometimes real life is almost the
   same,
as though you were being recited; you can almost tell what a thought
   is before it arrives.
When I follow my mind now, another butterfly happens. It's not hard
   to see why.
It's the country this time. The butterfly walked over the white table and
   onto my hand.
I lifted it and it held. My friends were amazed. Catherine tried, too, but
   the butterfly fluttered away.
I put my hand back in the air and it found me again. It came down on
   a finger and clung.
Its sails listed. I could see it untwirling the barb of its tongue on my
   nail. I shook it away.
Those were the days and the nights when Catherine and I were first
   falling in love.
Sometimes, in the dark, I'd still be afraid but she'd touch my arm and
   I'd sleep.
The visions I had then were all death: they were hideous and absurd
   and had nothing to do with my life.
All I feel now about death is a sadness, not to be here with everyone I
   love,
but in those days, I'd dream, I'd be wracked, Catherine would have to
   reach over to hold me.
In the morning, it would be better. Even at dawn, when I'd wake first,
   trembling, gasping for air,
I'd burrow back down, Catherine would open her eyes, smiling, with
   me at her breast, and it would be better.

The Shade

A summer cold. No rash. No fever. Nothing. But a dozen times during
the night I wake
to listen to my son whimpering in his sleep, trying to snort the sticky
phlegm out of his nostrils.
The passage clears, silence, nothing. I cross the room, groping for the
warm,
elusive creature of his breath and my heart lunges, stutters, tries to race
away;
I don't know from what, from my imagination, from life itself, maybe
from understanding too well
and being unable to do anything about how much of my anxiety is
always for myself.
Whatever it was, I left it when the dawn came. There's a park near here
where everyone who's out of work in our neighborhood comes to line
up in the morning.
The converted school buses shuttling hands to the cannery fields in Jersey
were just rattling away when I got there
and the small-time contractors, hiring out cheap walls, cheap ditches,
cheap everything,
were loading laborers onto the sacks of plaster and concrete in the backs
of their pickups.
A few housewives drove by looking for someone to babysit or clean
cellars for them,
then the gates of the local bar unlaced and whoever was left drifted in
out of the wall of heat
already rolling in with the first fists of smoke from the city incinerators.

It's so quiet now, I can hear the sparrows foraging scraps of garbage
on the paths.
The stove husk chained as a sign to the store across the street creaks in
the last breeze of darkness.
By noon, you'd have to be out of your mind to want to be here: the
park will reek of urine,

bodies will be sprawled on the benches, men will wrestle through the surf of broken bottles,
but even now, watching the leaves of the elms softly lifting toward the day, softly falling back,
all I see is fear forgiving fear on every page I turn; all I know is every time I try to change it,
I say it again: my wife, my child . . . my home, my work, my sorrow.
If this were the last morning of the world, if time had finally moved inside us and erupted
and we were Agamemnon again, Helen again, back on that faint, beginning planet
where even the daily survivals were giants, filled with light, I think I'd still be here,
afraid or not enough afraid, silently howling the names of death over the grass and asphalt.
The morning goes on, the sun burning, the earth burning, and between them, part of me lifts and starts back,
past the wash of dead music from the bar, the drinker reeling on the curb, the cars coughing alive,
and part, buried in itself, stays, forever, blinking into the glare, freezing.

With Ignorance

With ignorance begins a knowledge the first characteristic of which is ignorance.
—KIERKEGAARD

I

Again and again. Again lips, again breast, again hand, thigh, loin and
    bed and bed
after bed, the hunger, hunger again, need again, the rising, the spasm
    and needing again.
Flesh, lie, confusion and loathing, the scabs of clear gore, the spent seed
    and the spurt
of desire that seemed to generate from itself, from its own rising and
    spasm.
Everything waste, everything would be or was, the touching, the touch
    and the touch back.
Everything rind, scar, without sap, without meaning or seed, and every-
    one, everyone else,
every slip or leap into rage, every war, flame, sob, it was there, too, the
    stifling, the hushed,
malevolent frenzy and croak of desire, again and again, the same hunger,
    same need.
Touch me, hold me, sorrow and sorrow, the emptied, emptied again,
    touched again.
The hunger, the rising, again and again until again itself seemed to be
    need and hunger
and so much terror could rise out of that, the hunger repeating itself
    out of the fear now,
that how could you know if you lived within it at all, if there wasn't
    another,
a malediction or old prayer, a dream or a city of dream or a single,
    fleshless, dreamless error,
whose tongue you were, who spoke with you, butted or rasped with
    you, but still, tongue or another,
word or not word, what could it promise that wouldn't drive us back
    to the same hunger and sorrow?

What could it say that wouldn't spasm us back to ourselves to be bait
 or a dead prayer?
Or was that it? Only that? The prayer hunting its prey, hunting the bait
 of itself?
Was the hunger the faith in itself, the belief in itself, even the prayer?
Was it the dead prayer?

2

The faces waver; each gathers the others within it, the others shuddering
 through it
as though there were tides or depths, as though the depths, the tides of
 the eyes themselves
could throw out refractions, waves, shifts and wavers and each faceless
 refraction
could rise to waver beneath me, to shift, to be faceless again, beneath
 or within me,
the lying, confusion, recurrence, reluctance, the surge through into again.
Each room, each breast finding its ripeness of shadow, each lip and its
 shadow,
the dimming, flowing, the waver through time, through loss, gone,
 irredeemable,
all of it, each face into regret, each room into forgetting and absence.
But still, if there were a moment, still, one moment, to begin in or go
 back to,
to return to move through, waver through, only a single moment carved
 back from the lie
the way the breast is carved from its shadow, sealed from the dross of
 darkness
until it takes the darkness itself and fills with it, taking the breath;
if, in the return, I could be taken the way I could have been taken, with
 voice or breast,
emptied against the space of the breast as though breast was breath and
 my breath,
taken, would have been emptied into the moment, it could rise here,
 now, in that moment, the same moment.

But it won't, doesn't. The moments lift and fall, break, and it shifts,
   wavers,
subsides into the need again, the faceless again, the faceless and the lie.

3

Remorse? Blame? There is a pit-creature. The father follows it down
   with the ax.
Exile and sorrow. Once there were things we lived in, don't you
   remember?
We scraped, starved, then we came up, abashed, to the sun, and what
   was the first word?
Blame, blame and remorse, then sorrow, then the blame was the father
   then was ourselves.
Such a trite story, do we have to retell it? The mother took back the
   sun and we . . .
Remorse, self-regard, call it shame or being abashed or trying again, for
   the last time, to return.
Remorse, then power, the power and the blame and what did we ever
   suffer but power?
The head lifting itself, then the wars, remorse and revenge, the wars of
   humility,
the blades and the still valley, the double intention, the simple tree in
   the blood.
Then exile again, even the sword, even the spear, the formula scratched
   on the sand,
even the christening, the christened, blame again, power again, but even
   then,
taken out of the fire at the core and never returned, what could we not
   sanction?
One leg after the other, the look back, the power, the fire again and the
   sword again.
Blame and remorse. That gives into desire again, into hunger again. That
   gives into . . . this . . .

4

Someone . . . Your arm touches hers or hers finds yours, unmoving, unasking.

A silence, as though for the first time, and as though for the first time, you can listen,

as though there were chords: your life, then the other's, someone else, as though for the first time.

The life of the leaves over the streetlamp and the glow, swelling, chording, under the shadows,

and the quaver of things built, one quavering cell at a time, and the song

of the cell gently bedding itself in its mortar, in this silence, this first attempting.

Even the shush of cars, the complex stress of a step, the word called into the darkness,

and, wait, the things even beyond, beyond membrane or awareness, mode, sense, dream,

don't they sing, too? Chord, too? Isn't the song and the silence there, too?

I heard it once. It changed nothing, but once, before I went on, I did hear:

the equation of star and plant, the wheel, the ecstasy and division, the equation again.

The absolute walking its planks, its long wall, its long chord of laughter or grief.

I heard silence, then the children, the spawn, how we have to teach every cell how to speak,

and from that, after that, the kiss back from the speech, the touch back from the song.

And then more, I heard how it alters, how we, the speakers, the can't-live, the refuse-to,

how we, only in darkness, groaning and thrashing into the undergrowth of our eternal,

would speak then, would howl, howl again, and at last, at the end, we'd hear it:

the prayer and the flesh crying *Why aren't you here?* And the cry back in it, *I am! I am!*

5

Imagine dread. Imagine, without symbol, without figure, history or his-
tories; a place, not a place.
Imagine it must be risen through, beginning with the silent moment, the
secrets quieted,
one hour, one age at a time, sadness, nostalgia, the absurd pain of
betrayal.
Through genuine grief, then, through the genuine suffering for the
boundaries of self
and the touch on the edge, the compassion, that never, never quite,
breaks through.
Imagine the touch again and beyond it, beyond either end, joy or terror,
either ending,
the context that gives way, not to death, but past, past anything still
with a name,
even death, because even death is a promise offering comfort, solace,
that any direction we turn,
there'll still be the word, the name, and this the promise now, even with
terror,
the promise again that the wordlessness and the self won't be for one
instant the same enacting,
and we stay within it, a refusal now, a turning away, a never giving
way,
we stay until even extinction itself, the absence, death itself, even death,
isn't longed for,
never that, but turned toward in the deepest turn of the self, the deepest
gesture toward self.
And then back, from the dread, from locution and turn, from whatever
history reflects us,
the self grounds itself again in itself and reflects itself, even its loss, as
its own,
and back again, still holding itself back, the certainty and belief tearing
again,
back from the edge of that one flood of surrender which, given space,
would, like space itself,
rage beyond any limit, the flesh itself giving way in its terror, and back
from that,

into love, what we have to call love, the one moment before we move
    onwards again,
toward the end, the life again of the self-willed, self-created, embodied,
    reflected again.
Imagine a space prepared for with hunger, with dread, with power and
    the power
over dread which is dread, and the love, with no space for itself, no
    power for itself,
a moment, a silence, a rising, the terror for that, the space for that.
    Imagine love.

6

Morning. The first morning of now. You, your touch, your song and
    morning, but still,
something, a last fear or last lie or last clench of confusion clings,
holds back, refuses, resists, the way fear itself clings in its web of need
    or dread.
What would release be? Being forgiven? No, never forgiven, never only
    forgiven.
To be touched, somehow, with presence, so that the only sign is a step,
    towards or away?
Or not even a step, because the walls, of self, of dread, can never release,
can never forgive stepping away, out of the willed or refused, out of the
    lie or the fear
of the self that still holds back and refuses, resists, and turns back again
    and again into the willed.
What if it could be, though? The first, hectic rush past guilt or remorse?
What if we could find a way through the fires that aren't with us and
    the terrors that are?
What would be there? Would we be thrown back into perhaps or not
    yet or not needed or done?
Could we even slip back, again, past the first step into the first refusal,
the first need, first blot of desire that still somehow exists and wants to
    resist, wants to give back the hard,
immaculate shell of the terror it still keeps against respite and
    unclenching?
Or perhaps no release, no step or sign, perhaps only to wait and accept.

Perhaps only to bless. To bless and to bless and to bless and to bless.

Willed or unwilled, word or sign, the word suddenly filled with its own breath.

Self and other the self within other and the self still moved through its word,

consuming itself, still, and consuming, still being rage, war, the fear, the aghast,

but bless, bless still, even the fear, the loss, the gutting of word, the gutting even of hunger,

but still to bless and bless, even the turn back, the refusal, to bless and to bless and to bless.

7

The first language was loss, the second sorrow, this is the last, then: yours . . .

An island, summer, late dusk; hills, laurel and thorn. I walked from the harbor, over the cliff road,

down the long trail through the rocks. When I came to our house the ship's wake was just edging onto the shore

and on the stone beach, under the cypress, the low waves reassuming themselves in the darkness, I waited.

There was a light in a room. You came to it, leaned to it, reaching, touching,

and watching you, I saw you give back to the light a light more than light

and to the silence you gave more than silence, and, in the silence, I heard it.

You, your self, your life, your beginning, pleasure, song clear as the light that touched you.

Your will, your given and taken; grief, recklessness, need, or desire.

Your passion or tear, step forward or step back into the inevitable veil.

Yours and yours and yours, the dream, the wall of the self that won't be or needn't be breached,

and the breach, the touch, yours and the otherness, yours, the separateness,

never giving way, never breached really, but as simple, always, as light, as silence.

This is the language of that, that light and that silence, the silence rising
     through or from you.
Nothing to bless or not bless now, nothing to thank or forgive, not to
     triumph,
surrender, mean, reveal, assume or exhaust. Our faces bent to the light,
     and still,
there is terror, still history, power, grief and remorse, always, always
     the self and the other
and the endless tide, the waver, the terror again, between and beneath,
     but you, now,
your touch, your light, the otherness yours, the reach, the wheel, the
     waves touching.
And to, not wait, not overcome, not even forget or forgive the dream
     of the moment, the unattainable moment again.
Your light . . . Your silence . . .
In the silence, without listening, I heard it, and without words, without
     language or breath, I answered.

Tar

From My Window

Spring: the first morning when that one true block of sweet, laminar,
    complex scent arrives
from somewhere west and I keep coming to lean on the sill, glorying in
    the end of the wretched winter.
The scabby-barked sycamores ringing the empty lot across the way are
    budded—I hadn't noticed—
and the thick spikes of the unlikely urban crocuses have already broken
    the gritty soil.
Up the street, some surveyors with tripods are waving each other left
    and right the way they do.
A girl in a gym suit jogged by a while ago, some kids passed, playing
    hooky, I imagine,
and now the paraplegic Vietnam vet who lives in a half-converted ware-
    house down the block
and the friend who stays with him and seems to help him out come
    weaving towards me,
their battered wheelchair lurching uncertainly from one edge of the
    sidewalk to the other.
I know where they're going—to the "Legion": once, when I was putting
    something out, they stopped,
both drunk that time, too, both reeking—it wasn't ten o'clock—and we
    chatted for a bit.
I don't know how they stay alive—on benefits most likely. I wonder if
    they're lovers?
They don't look it. Right now, in fact, they look a wreck, careening
    haphazardly along,
contriving, as they reach beneath me, to dip a wheel from the curb so
    that the chair skewers, teeters,
tips, and they both tumble, the one slowly, almost gracefully sliding in
    stages from his seat,
his expression hardly marking it, the other staggering over him, spinning
    heavily down,
to lie on the asphalt, his mouth working, his feet shoving weakly and
    fruitlessly against the curb.

In the storefront office on the corner, Reed and Son, Real Estate, have come to see the show.

Gazing through the golden letters of their name, they're not, at least, thank god, laughing.

Now the buddy, grabbing at a hydrant, gets himself erect and stands there for a moment, panting.

Now he has to lift the other one, who lies utterly still, a forearm shielding his eyes from the sun.

He hauls him partly upright, then hefts him almost all the way into the chair, but a dangling foot

catches a support-plate, jerking everything around so that he has to put him down,

set the chair to rights, and hoist him again and as he does he jerks the grimy jeans right off him.

No drawers, shrunken, blotchy thighs: under the thick, white coils of belly blubber,

the poor, blunt pud, tiny, terrified, retracted, is almost invisible in the sparse genital hair,

then his friend pulls his pants up, he slumps wholly back as though he were, at last, to be let be,

and the friend leans against the cyclone fence, suddenly staring up at me as though he'd known,

all along, that I was watching and I can't help wondering if he knows that in the winter, too,

I watched, the night he went out to the lot and walked, paced rather, almost ran, for how many hours.

It was snowing, the city in that holy silence, the last we have, when the storm takes hold,

and he was making patterns that I thought at first were circles, then realized made a figure eight,

what must have been to him a perfect symmetry but which, from where I was, shivered, bent,

and lay on its side: a warped, unclear infinity, slowly, as the snow came faster, going out.

Over and over again, his head lowered to the task, he slogged the path he'd blazed,

but the race was lost, his prints were filling faster than he made them now and I looked away,

up across the skeletal trees to the tall center city buildings, some, though
    it was midnight,
with all their offices still gleaming, their scarlet warning beacons signaling
    erratically
against the thickening flakes, their smoldering auras softening portions
    of the dim, milky sky.
In the morning, nothing: every trace of him effaced, all the field pure
    white,
its surface glittering, the dawn, glancing from its glaze, oblique, relent-
    less, unadorned.

My Mother's Lips

Until I asked her to please stop doing it and was astonished to find that
      she not only could
but from the moment I asked her in fact would stop doing it, my mother,
      all through my childhood,
when I was saying something to her, something important, would move
      her lips as I was speaking
so that she seemed to be saying under her breath the very words I was
      saying as I was saying them.

Or, even more disconcertingly—wildly so now that my puberty had
      erupted—*before* I said them.
When I was smaller, I must just have assumed that she was omniscient.
      Why not?
She knew everything else—when I was tired, or lying; she'd know I was
      ill before I did.
I may even have thought—how could it not have come into my mind?
      —that she *caused* what I said.

All she was really doing of course was mouthing my words a split second
      after I said them myself,
but it wasn't until my own children were learning to talk that I really
      understood how,
and understood, too, the edge of anxiety in it, the wanting to bring you
      along out of the silence,
the compulsion to lift you again from those blank caverns of nameless-
      ness we encase.

That was long afterward, though: where I was now was just wanting
      to get her to stop,
and, considering how I brooded and raged in those days, how quickly
      my teeth went on edge,
the restraint I approached her with seems remarkable, although her so
      unprotestingly,

readily taming a habit by then three children and a dozen years old was
 as much so.

It's endearing to watch us again in that long-ago dusk, facing each other,
 my mother and me.
I've just grown to her height, or just past it: there are our lips moving
 together,
now the unison suddenly breaks, I have to go on by myself, no maestro,
 no score to follow.
I wonder what finally made me take umbrage enough, or heart enough,
 to confront her?

It's not important. My cocoon at that age was already unwinding: the
 threads ravel and snarl.
When I find one again, it's that two o'clock in the morning, a grim hotel
 on a square,
the impenetrable maze of an endless city, when, really alone for the first
 time in my life,
I found myself leaning from the window, incanting in a tearing whisper
 what I thought were poems.

I'd love to know what I raved that night to the night, what those innocent
 dithyrambs were,
or to feel what so ecstatically drew me out of myself and beyond . . .
 Nothing is there, though,
only the solemn piazza beneath me, the riot of dim, tiled roofs and
 impassable alleys,
my desolate bed behind me, and my voice, hoarse, and the sweet, alien
 air against me like a kiss.

The Dog

Except for the dog, that she wouldn't have him put away, wouldn't let
    him die, I'd have liked her.
She was handsome, busty, chunky, early middle-aged, very black, with
    a stiff, exotic dignity
that flurried up in me a mix of warmth and sexual apprehension neither
    of which, to tell the truth,
I tried very hard to nail down: she was that much older and in those
    days there was still the race thing.
This was just at the time of civil rights: the neighborhood I was living
    in was mixed.
In the narrow streets, the tiny three-floored houses they called father-
    son-holy-ghosts
which had been servants' quarters first, workers' tenements, then slums,
    still were, but enclaves of us,
beatniks and young artists, squatted there and commerce between every-
    one was fairly easy.
Her dog, a grinning mongrel, rib and knob, gristle and grizzle, wasn't
    terribly offensive.
The trouble was that he was ill, or the trouble more exactly was that I
    had to know about it.
She used to walk him on a lot I overlooked, he must have had a tumor
    or a blockage of some sort
because every time he moved his bowels, he shrieked, a chilling, almost
    human scream of anguish.
It nearly always caught me unawares, but even when I'd see them first,
    it wasn't better.
The limp leash coiled in her hand, the woman would be profiled to the
    dog, staring into the distance,
apparently oblivious, those breasts of hers like stone, while he, not a
    step away, laboring,
trying to eject the feeble, mucus-coated, blood-flecked chains that finally
    spurted from him,
would set himself on tiptoe and hump into a question mark, one quiv-
    ering back leg grotesquely lifted.

Every other moment he'd turn his head, as though he wanted her, to
    no avail, to look at him,
then his eyes would dim and he'd drive his wounded anus in the dirt,
    keening uncontrollably,
lurching forward in a hideous, electric dance as though someone were
    at him with a club.
When at last he'd finish, she'd wipe him with a tissue like a child; he'd
    lick her hand.
It was horrifying; I was always going to call the police; once I actually
    went out to chastise her—
didn't she know how selfish she was, how the animal was suffering?—
    she scared me off, though.
She was older than I'd thought, for one thing, her flesh was loosening,
    pouches of fat beneath the eyes,
and poorer, too, shabby, tarnished: I imagined smelling something
    faintly acrid as I passed.
Had I ever really mooned for such a creature? I slunk around the block,
    chagrined, abashed.
I don't recall them too long after that. Maybe the dog died, maybe I
    was just less sensitive.
Maybe one year when the cold came and I closed my windows, I forgot
    them . . . then I moved.
Everything was complicated now, so many tensions, so much bother-
    some self-consciousness.
Anyway, those back streets, especially in bad weather when the ginkgos
    lost their leaves, were bleak.
It's restored there now, ivy, pointed brick, garden walls with broken
    bottles mortared on them,
but you'd get sick and tired then: the rubbish in the gutter, the general
    sense of dereliction.
Also, I'd found a girl to be in love with: all we wanted was to live
    together, so we did.

The Color of Time

Although the lamp is out, and although it's dusk, late, dull, stifling
    summer dusk,
a wash of the column of grimy light reflects from the airshaft the boy's
    bedroom faces:
he can still make out his model bomber twisting and untwisting on its
    thread from the ceiling.
Everything else is utterly still. The air, breathed, breathed again, is thick,
    decomposed,
a dense, almost organic, almost visible volume of soiled grains suspended
    in the liquid heat.
The boy, in briefs and T-shirt, his limp sheet disarrayed, sweats lightly,
    not disagreeably—
his frictionless skin and the complex savor at the corners of his mouth
    intrigue him.
Suddenly, outside, a few feet away, a voice, a woman's, harsh but af-
    fectless, droning.
"I can't go on," it says. Pause. Then, more fervor, more conviction:
    I can't go on.
The boy looks across: the window on the other side of the shaft, a blur
    of uncertain amber,
its panes streaked as though someone had swiped a greasy rag across
    them, is shut,
the yellowed paint on the rotting sill beneath it has bubbled and scabbed
    in erratic strips.
More plaintively now, almost whining, "You're drunk," the voice says,
    "You're drunk, aren't you?"
Everything twice, the boy notes. His mother and father are out. What
    time must it be?
"I'm beating my head." The boy lifts in a more focused, more definite
    interest this time.
Pause. *I'm beating my head*, the voice at last reaffirms. A door crashes
    somewhere.
The boy has only infrequently seen the woman: out back, by the trash,
    sometimes they pass,

but her image is vivid—slippers, a housedress with a lifeless nightgown
hanging under the hem.

Something about her repels the boy, maybe the nightgown, maybe that
their eyes never meet.

Nothing now. The boy's testicles somehow have slipped out of the leg
of his shorts.

Awkwardly, he tucks them back in: how wrinkled they are, the skin
tougher than the soles of his feet.

Later, the boy sits up. Has he been sleeping? The night seems stricter,
the other window is dark.

The boy knows that sometimes he wakes: the next morning his mother
will say with exasperation,

"You woke up screaming again," and sometimes he'll remember her
arms or his father's around him.

He never remembers the scream, just the embrace, usually not even that,
but once, he knows,

he called out, his father came to him: *Listen*, the boy said, *outside, there
are babies crying.*

Cats, his father, angry beyond what the occasion seemed to imply, had
whispered, *Go to sleep*,

jerking roughly, irrationally, the boy had thought, the sheet up nearly
over the boy's head.

Although it's quiet now, not a sound, it's hard—the boy doesn't know
why—not to cry out.

He tries to imagine the bar of warm glow from his parents' room bi-
secting the hall

but the darkness stays stubbornly intact and whatever it is shuddering
in his chest keeps on.

I hope I don't cry, he thinks; his thighs lock over his fists: he can hold
it, he thinks.

Flight

The last party before I left was in an old, run-down apartment house,
 The Greystone Arms,
the owners of which were involved in a drawn-out legal wrangle with
 some of the tenants.
The building was to be razed and redeveloped, the tenants, mostly older
 women who'd lived there forever,
were contesting being evicted—I forget on what grounds—and in the
 meantime everyone else had vacated
and the apartments had been rented to anyone who'd take them month-
 to-month, without leases.
The party when I heard about it had apparently been going on all night
 every night for weeks
in the penthouse a few hippie types I knew vaguely and didn't particularly
 care for had taken over.
I was tempted anyway: this was still the sixties when if anything was
 happening, you went,
besides, I was at loose ends, and, although I didn't like admitting it,
 chronically adrift and lonely.
I'd been curious about the Greystone, I could tell myself that all I wanted
 was to get inside.
The exterior had mostly kept its splendors, brass fittings, carved stone
 urns and lintels:
even the grisly old awning still somehow hung together, though all it
 seemed ever to shelter now
was the congregation of tranquillized ex-mental patients whose agencies
 had parked them in the building
and who you'd see huddled there, day and the down and out dead of
 night, nowhere to go, nothing to do,
shuffling dreamily aside when the speed-freaks and junkies would flit
 out to make their hits
or when the ladies who still were living in all this would huff past into
 the dilapidated lobby.
The ladies: that they'd have wanted to stay on at all by now was a
 triumph of pure indignation,

the place was crawling down so fast, but they hung on, barricaded in
    their genteel cubicles.
How dire it must have been for them—the hallways with bare, under-
    watted fixtures,
the rotten plumbing booming through the night, the hiss of the addicts
    outside their doors.
Whatever elegance there might have been was eaten by neglect: the
    wallpaper hung in ratty strips,
its ribbons and roses had bled through onto the ocher plaster underneath
    and everything,
even the palsied elevator, emitted the spermy, scummy odor of half a
    century of secret damp.
The penthouse, up an extra flight of filthy stairs, was as bad, and the
    party, if possible, was worse.
Every misfit in the city, every freeloader, every blown-out druggie and
    glazed teenybopper
plus the crazies from the building and no telling who or what else had
    filtered up there.
Stunned on rotgut wine or grass or acid, they danced mechanically in
    the daze of the deafening music,
or sprawled on the floor, offhandedly fumbling at one another as though
    no one else was in the room.
There was something almost maniacally mindless about it, but at the
    same time it was like a battle,
that intense, that lunatic, and, hesitating in the doorway, something
    made me realize just how much
without noticing I'd come to be of that, to want or need it, and I swear
    I must have swayed,
the way, over their imaginary chaos, Manfred must have swayed, and
    Faust, before it swallowed them.

There's a park there now. The morning I came back, I wandered by and
    stopped to sit awhile.
Why, after all the fuss, a park, I don't know, but at any rate, it's not a
    pleasant place,
reinforced, bleak concrete mostly; a fountain, ringed with granite, out
    of order, dry.

Two busloads of retarded kids were playing with their teachers on the
    asphalt ball field,
twittering with glee and shrieking as they lumbered from home plate to
    center field and back.
A whole platoon of them, the smallest ones—adorable—had imitation
    football helmets.
Some food chain's plastic giveaways, the things had eagles stenciled on
    them, and the letters GIANTS.
The other benches were populated with old women, the Greystone ladies,
    back to claim their turf, I thought.
It was mild and sunny. I let my eyes close, and dozed and dreamed,
    listening to the children.

The Gift

I have found what pleases my friend's chubby, rosy, gloriously shining-
    eyed year-old daughter.
She chirps, flirts with me, pulls herself up by my pants leg, and her
    pleasure is that I lift her,
high, by her thighs, over my head, and then that I let her suddenly fall,
    plunge, plummet,
down through my hands, to be, at the last instant, under the arms, in
    mid-gasp, caught.
She laughs when I do it, she giggles, roars; she is flushed with it, glowing,
    elated, ecstatic.
When I put her down, she whines, whimpers, claws at my lap: *Again*,
    she is saying . . . *Again: More.*
I pick up my glass, though, my friend and I chat, the child keeps at me
    but I pay no mind.

Once I would never have done that, released her like that, not until,
    satisfied, sated,
no need left, no "more," nothing would have been left for her but to
    fold sighing in my arms.
Once it was crucial that I be able to think of myself as unusually gifted
    with children.
And, even discounting the effort I put in it all, the premeditation, the
    scheming, I was.
I'd studied what they would want—at this age to rise, to fall, be tickled,
    caressed.
Older, to be heeded, attended: I had stories, dreams, ways to confide,
    take confidence back.
But beyond that, children did love me, I think, and beyond that, there
    seemed more.

I could calm crying babies, even when they were furious, shrieking, the
    mothers at wit's end.
I had rituals I'd devised, whisperings, clicks; soft, blowy whistles, a song-
    voice.

A certain firmness of hand, I remember I thought: concentration, a
    deepening of the gaze.
Maybe they'd be surprised to find me with them at all instead of the
    mother or father,
but, always, they'd stop, sometimes so abruptly, with such drama, that
    even I would be taken aback.
Tears, sometimes, would come to my eyes: I would be flooded with
    thanks that I'd been endowed with this,
or had resurrected it from some primitive source of grace I imagined
    we'd bartered away.

What else did I have then? Not very much: being alone most of the time,
    retrospectively noble,
but bitter back then, brutal, abrasive, corrosive—I was wearing away
    with it like a tooth.
And my sexual hunger, how a breast could destroy me, or a haunch:
    not having the beautiful haunch.
. . . And love, too, I suppose, yes, now and then, for a girl, never for
    other men's wives yet . . .
Where did the children fit in, though, that odd want to entrance and
    enchant, to give bliss?
Did no one think I was mad? Didn't I ever wonder myself if I was using
    the children,
whether needs or compulsions, at least sublimations, were unaccounted
    for in my passion?

No, never, more sense to ask if those vulnerable creatures of the heart
    used me.
The children were light—I thought they pertained to my wish to be pure,
    a saint.
I never conjoined them with anything else, not with the loneliness or
    the vile desire,
not with my rages nor the weary, nearly irrepressible urges I'd feel to
    let go, to die.
The children were light, or let intimations of light through—they were
    the way to the soul:

I wanted to think myself, too, a matrix of innocent warmth instead of
    the sorrowing brute I was,
stumbling out by myself into the moaning darkness again, thrust again
    into that murderous prowl.

On Learning of a Friend's Illness

FOR JAMES WRIGHT

The morning is so gray that the grass is gray and the side of the white
    horse grazing
is as gray and hard as the harsh, insistent wind gnawing the iron surface
    of the river,
while far off on the other shore, the eruptions from the city seem for
    once more docile and benign
than the cover of nearly indistinguishable clouds they unfurl to insinuate
    themselves among.

It is a long while since the issues of mortality have taken me this way.
    Shivering,
I tramp the thin, bitten track to the first rise, the first descent, and, toiling
    up again,
I startle out of their brushy hollow the whole herd of wild-eyed, shaggy,
    unkempt mares,
their necks, rumps, withers, even faces begrimed with patches of the
    gluey, alluvial mud.

All of them at once, their nostrils flared, their tails flung up over their
    backs like flags,
are suddenly in flight, plunging and shoving along the narrow furrow
    of the flood ditch,
bursting from its mouth, charging headlong toward the wires at the
    pasture's end,
banking finally like one great, graceful wing to scatter down the hillside
    out of sight.

Only the oldest of them all stays with me, and she, sway-backed, over
    at the knees,
blind, most likely deaf, still, when I move towards her, swings her meager
    backside to me,
her ears flattening, the imperturbable opals of her eyes gazing resolutely
    over the bare,

scruffy fields, the scattered pines and stands of third-growth oak I called
    a forest once.

I slip up on her, hook her narrow neck, haul her to me, hold her for a
    moment, let her go.
I hardly can remember anymore what there ever was out here that keeps
    me coming back
to watch the land be amputated by freeways and developments, and the
    mares, in their sanctuary,
thinning out, reverting, becoming less and less approachable, more and
    more the symbols of themselves.

How cold it is. The hoofprints in the hardened muck are frozen lakes,
    their rims atilt,
their glazed opacities skewered with straw, muddled with the ancient
    and ubiquitous manure.
I pick a morsel of it up: scentless, harmless, cool, as desiccated as an
    empty hive,
it crumbles in my hand, its weightless, wingless filaments taken from
    me by the wind and strewn

in a long, surprising arc that wavers once then seems to burst into a
    rain of dust.
No comfort here, nothing to say, to try to say, nothing for anyone. I
    start the long trek back,
the horses nowhere to be seen, the old one plodding wearily away to
    join them,
the river, bitter to look at, and the passionless earth, and the grasses
    rushing ceaselessly in place.

Combat

Ich hatte einst ein schönes Vaterland . . . Es war ein Traum.
—HEINRICH HEINE

I've been trying for hours to figure out who I was reminded of by the
    welterweight fighter
I saw on television this afternoon all but ruin his opponent with counter-
    punches and now I have it.
It was a girl I knew once, a woman: when he was being interviewed
    after the knockout, he was her exactly,
the same rigorous carriage, same facial structure—sharp cheekbones,
    very vivid eyebrows—
even the sheen of perspiration—that's how I'd remember her, of course
    . . . Moira was her name—
and the same quality in the expression of unabashed self-involvement,
    softened at once with a grave,
almost oversensitive attentiveness to saying with absolute precision what
    was to be said.
Lovely Moira! Could I ever have forgotten you? No, not forgotten, only
    not had with me for a time
that dark, slow voice, those vulnerable eyes, those ankles finely tendoned
    as a thoroughbred's.
We met I don't remember where—everything that mattered happened
    in her apartment, in the living room,
with her mother, whom she lived with, watching us, and in Moira's
    bedroom down the book-lined corridor.
The mother, I remember, was so white, not all that old but white:
    everything, hair, skin, lips, was ash,
except her feet, which Moira would often hold on her lap to massage
    and which were a deep,
frightening yellow, the skin thickened and dense, horned with calluses
    and chains of coarse, dry bunions,
the nails deformed and brown, so deeply buried that they looked like
    chips of tortoiseshell.
Moira would rub the poor, sad things, twisting and kneading at them
    with her strong hands;

the mother's eyes would be closed, occasionally she'd mutter something
under her breath in German.

That was their language—they were, Moira said, refugees, but the word
didn't do them justice.

They were well-off, very much so, their apartment was, in fact, the most
splendid thing I'd ever seen.

There were lithographs and etchings—some Klees, I think; a Munch—
a lot of very flat oriental rugs,

voluptuous leather furniture and china so frail the molds were surely
cast from butterflies.

I never found out how they'd brought it all with them: what Moira told
me was of displaced-person camps,

a pilgrimage on foot from Prussia and the Russians, then Frankfurt,
Rotterdam, and here, "freedom."

The trip across the war was a complicated memory for her; she'd been
very young, just in school,

what was most important to her at that age was her father, who she'd
hardly known and who'd just died.

He was a general, she told me, the chief of staff or something of "the
war against the Russians."

He'd been one of the conspirators against Hitler and when the plot failed
he'd committed suicide,

all of which meant not very much to me, however good the story was
(and I heard it often),

because people then were still trying to forget the war, it had been almost
ignored, even in school,

and I had no context much beyond what my childhood comic books
had given me to hang any of it on.

Moira was fascinated by it, though, and by their journey, and whenever
she wanted to offer me something—

when I'd despair, for instance, of ever having from her what I had to
have—it would be, again, that tale.

In some ways it was, I think, her most precious possession, and every
time she'd unfold it

she'd seem to have forgotten having told me before: each time the images
would be the same—

a body by the roadside, a child's—awful—her mother'd tried to hide
her eyes but she'd jerked free;

a white ceramic cup of sweet, cold milk in the dingy railroad station of
     some forgotten city,
then the boat, the water, black, the webs of rushing foam she'd made
     up creatures for, who ran beneath the waves
and whose occupation was to snare the boat, to snarl it, then . . . she
     didn't know what then,
and I'd be hardly listening anyway by then, one hand on a thigh, the
     other stroking,
with such compassion, such generous concern, such cunning twenty-
     one-year-old commiseration,
her hair, her perfect hair, then the corner of her mouth, then, so far
     away, the rich rim of a breast.
We'd touch that way—petting was the word then—like lovers, with the
     mother right there with us,
probably, I remember thinking, because we weren't lovers, not really,
     not *that* way (not yet, I'd think),
but beyond that there seemed something else, some complicity between
     them, some very adult undertaking
that I sensed but couldn't understand and that astonished me as did
     almost everything about them.
I never really liked the mother—I was never given anything to like—but
     I was awed by her.
If I was left alone with her—Moira on the phone, say—I stuttered, or
     was stricken mute.
It felt like I was sitting there with time itself: everything seemed somehow
     finished for her,
but there seemed, still, to be such depths, or such ascensions, to her
     unblinking brooding.
She was like a footnote to a text, she seemed to know it, suffer it, and,
     if I was wildly uneasy with her,
my eyes battering shyly in their chutes, it was my own lack, my own
     unworthiness that made it so.
Moira would come back, we'd talk again, I can't imagine what about
     except, again, obsessively, the father,
his dying, his estates, the stables, servants, all they'd given up for the
     madness of that creature Hitler.
I'd listen to it all again, and drift, looking in her eyes, and pine, pondering
     her lips.

I knew that I was dying of desire—down of cheek; subtle, alien scent—
    that I'd never felt desire like this.
I was so distracted that I couldn't even get their name right: they'd kept
    the real pronunciation,
I'd try to ape what I remembered of my grandmother's Polish Yiddish
    but it still eluded me
and Moira's little joke before she'd let me take her clothes off was that
    we'd have lessons, "Von C . . ." "No, Von C . . ."
Later, when I was studying the holocaust, I found it again, the name,
    Von C . . . , in Shirer's *Reich*:
it had, indeed, existed, and it had, yes, somewhere on the Eastern front,
    blown its noble head off.
I wasn't very moved. I wasn't in that city anymore, I'd ceased long before
    ever to see them,
and besides, I'd changed by then—I was more aware of history and was
    beginning to realize,
however tardily, that one's moral structures tended to be air unless you
    grounded them in real events.
Everything I did learn seemed to negate something else, everything was
    more or less up for grabs,
but the war, the Germans, all I knew about that now—no, never: what
    a complex triumph to have a nation,
all of it, beneath you, what a splendid culmination for the adolescence
    of one's ethics!
As for Moira, as for her mother, what recompense for those awful hours,
    those ecstatic unaccomplishments.
I reformulated her—them—forgave them, held them fondly, with a heavy
    lick of condescension, in my system.
But for now, there we are, Moira and I, down that hall again, in her
    room again, both with nothing on.
I can't say what she looked like. I remember that I thought her somewhat
    too robust, her chest too thick,
but I was young, and terrified, and quibbled everything: now, no doubt,
    I'd find her perfect.
In my mind now, naked, she's almost too much so, too blond, too gold,
    her pubic hair, her arm and leg fur,
all of it is brushed with light, so much glare she seems to singe the very
    tissue of remembrance,

but there are—I can see them now and didn't then—promises of dimness, vaults and hidden banks of coolness.

If I couldn't, though, appreciate the subtleties, it wasn't going to hold me back, no, it was *she* who held me back,

always, as we struggled on that narrow bed, twisted on each other, mauling one another like demented athletes.

So fierce it was, so strenuous, aggressive: my thigh *here*, my hand *here*, lips *here*, *here*,

hers *here* and *here* but never *there* or *there* . . . before it ended, she'd have even gone into the sounds of love,

groans and whispered shrieks, glottal stops, gutturals I couldn't catch or understand,

and all this while *nothing would be happening*, nothing, that is, in the way I'd mean it now.

We'd lie back (this is where I see her sweating, gleaming with it, drenched) and she'd smile.

She is satisfied somehow. This is what she wanted somehow. Only this? Yes, only this,

and we'd be back, that quickly, in my recollection anyway, with the mother in the other room,

the three of us in place, the conversation that seemed sometimes like a ritual, eternally recurring.

How long we were to wait like this was never clear to me; my desperation, though, was slow in gathering.

I must have liked the role, or the pretense of the role, of beast, primed, about to pounce,

and besides, her hesitations, her fendings-off, were so warm and so bewildering,

I was so engrossed in them, that when at last, once and for all, she let me go,

the dismissal was so adroitly managed that I never realized until perhaps right now

that what had happened wasn't my own coming to the conclusion that this wasn't worth the bother.

It's strange now, doing it again, the business of the camps and slaughters, the quick flicker of outrage

that hardly does its work anymore, all the carnage, all our own omissions interposed,

then those two, in their chambers, correct, aristocratic, even with the
old one's calcifying feet
and the younger one's intensities—those eyes that pierce me still from
that far back with jolts of longing.
I frame the image: the two women, the young man, they, poised, gra-
cious, he smoldering with impatience,
and I realize I've never really asked myself what could she, or they,
possibly have wanted of me?
What am I doing in that room, a teacup trembling on my knee, that
odd, barbed name mangled in my mouth?
If she felt a real affinity or anything resembling it for me, it must have
been as something quaint—
young poet, brutish, or trying to be brutish—but no, I wasn't even that,
I was just a boy, harmless, awkward,
mildly appealing in some ways, I suppose, but certainly with not a thing
about me one could call compelling,
not compared to what, given her beauty and her means, she could have
had and very well may have, for all I knew.
What I come to now, running over it again, I think I want to keep as
undramatic as I can.
These revisions of the past are probably even less trustworthy than our
random, everyday assemblages
and have most likely even more to do with present unknowables, so I
offer this almost in passing,
with nothing, no moral distillation, no headily pressing imperatives
meant to be lurking beneath it.
I wonder, putting it most simply, leaving out humiliation, anything like
that, if I might have been their Jew?
I wonder, I mean, if I might have been an implement for them, not of
atonement—I'd have nosed that out—
but of absolution, what they'd have used to get them shed of something
rankling—history, it would be:
they'd have wanted to be categorically and finally shriven of it, or of
that part of it at least
which so befouled the rest, which so acutely contradicted it with glory
and debasement.
The mother, what I felt from her, that bulk of silence, that withholding
that I read as sorrow:

might it have been instead the heroic containment of a probably reflexive
    loathing of me?
How much, no matter what their good intentions (of which from her I
    had no evidence at all)
and even with the liberal husband (although the generals' reasons weren't
    that pure and got there very late),
how much must they have inevitably absorbed, that Nazi generation,
    those Aryan epochs?
And if the mother shuddered, what would Moira have gone through
    with me spinning at her nipple,
her own juices and the inept emissions I'd splatter on her gluing her to
    me?
The purifying Jew. It's almost funny. She was taking just enough of me
    to lave her conscience,
and I, so earnest in my wants, blindly labored for her, dismantling guilt
    or racial squeamishness
or whatever it was the refined tablet of her consciousness deemed it
    needed to be stricken of.
All the indignities I let be perpetrated on me while I lolled in that
    luxurious detention:
could I really have believed they only had to do with virtue, maidenhood,
    or even with, I remember thinking—
I came this close—some intricate attempt Moira might be making to
    redeem a slight on the part of the mother?
Or might inklings have arisen and might I, in my infatuation, have gone
    along with them anyway?
I knew something, surely: I'd have had to. What I really knew, of course,
    I'll never know again.
Beautiful memory, most precious and most treacherous sister: what
    temples must we build for you.
And even then, how belatedly you open to us; even then, with what
    exuberance you cross us.

Floor

A dirty picture, a photograph, possibly a tintype, from the turn of the
     century, even before:
the woman is obese, gigantic; a broad, black corset cuts from under her
     breasts to the top of her hips,
her hair is crimped, wiry, fastened demurely back with a bow one in-
     congruous wing of which shows.
Her eyebrows are straight and heavy, emphasizing her frank, unintro-
     spective plainness
and she looks directly, easily into the camera, her expression somewhere
     between play and scorn,
as though the activities of the photographer were ridiculous or beneath
     her contempt, or,
rather, as though the unfamiliar camera were actually the much more
     interesting presence here
and how absurd it is that the lens be turned toward her and her partner
     and not back on itself.
One sees the same look—pride, for some reason, is in it, and a surpris-
     ingly sophisticated self-distancing—
in the snaps anthropologists took in backwaters during those first, po-
     litically preconscious,
golden days of culture-hopping, and, as Goffman notes, in certain ad-
     vertisements, now.

The man is younger than the woman. Standing, he wears what looks
     like a bathing costume,
black and white tank top, heavy trousers bunched in an ungainly heap
     over his shoes, which are still on.
He has an immigrant's mustache he's a year or two too callow for, but,
     thick and dark, it will fit him.
He doesn't, like the woman, watch the camera, but stares ahead, not at
     the woman but slightly over and past,
and there's a kind of withdrawn, almost vulnerable thoughtfulness or
     preoccupation about him

despite the gross thighs cast on his waist and the awkward, surely both-
ersome twist

his body has been forced to assume to more clearly exhibit the genital
penetration.

He seems, in fact, abstracted—oblivious wouldn't be too strong a word—
as though, possibly,

as unlikely as it would seem, he had been a virgin until now and was
trying amid all this unholy confusion—

the hooded figure, the black box with its eye—trying, and from the looks
of it even succeeding

in obliterating everything from his consciousness but the thing itself, the
act itself,

so as, one would hope, to redeem the doubtlessly endless nights of the
long Victorian adolescence.

The background is a painted screen: ivy, columns, clouds; some muse
or grace or other,

heavy-buttocked, whory, flaunts her gauze and clodhops with a half-
demented leer.

The whole thing's oddly poignant somehow, almost, like an antique
wedding picture, comforting—

the past is sending out a tendril to us: poses, attitudes of stillness we've
lost or given back.

Also, there's no shame in watching them, in being in the tacit commerce
of having, like it or not,

received the business in one's hand, no titillation either, not a tangle,
not a throb,

probably because the woman offers none of the normal symptoms, even
if minimal, even if contrived—

the tongue, say, wandering from the corner of the mouth, a glint of
extra brilliance at the lash—

we associate to even the most innocuous, undramatic, parental sorts of
passion, and the boy,

well, dragged in out of history, off Broome or South Street, all he is is
grandpa:

he'll go back into whatever hole he's found to camp in, those higher-
contrast tenements

with their rows of rank, forbidding beds, or not even beds, rags on a
    floor, or floor.
On the way there, there'll be policemen breaking strikers' heads, or
    micks', or sheenies',
there'll be war somewhere, in the sweatshops girls will turn to stone
    over their Singers.
Here, at least peace. Here, one might imagine, after he withdraws, a
    kind of manly focus taking him—
the glance he shoots to her is hard and sure—and, to her, a tenderness
    might come,
she might reach a hand—Sweet Prince—to touch his cheek, or might—
    who can understand these things?—
avert her face and pull him to her for a time before she squats to flush
    him out.

Waking Jed

Deep asleep, perfect immobility, no apparent evidence of consciousness
    or of dream.
Elbow cocked, fist on pillow lightly curled to the tension of the partially
    relaxing sinew.
Head angled off, just so: the jaw's projection exaggerated slightly, almost
    to prognathous: why?
The features express nothing whatsoever and seem to call up no response
    in me.
Though I say nothing, don't move, gradually, far down within, he, or
    rather not *he* yet,
something, a presence, an element of being, becomes aware of me: there
    begins a subtle,
very gentle alteration in the structure of the face, or maybe less than
    that, more elusive,
as though the soft distortions of sleep-warmth radiating from his face
    and flesh,
those essentially unreal mirages in the air between us, were modifying,
    dissipating.
The face is now more his, Jed's—its participation in the almost Ro-
    manesque generality
I wouldn't a moment ago have been quite able to specify, not having
    its contrary, diminishes.
Particularly on the cheekbones and chin, the skin is thinning, growing
    denser, harder,
the molecules on the points of bone coming to attention, the eyelids
    finer, brighter, foil-like:
capillaries, veins; though nothing moves, there are goings to and fro
    behind now.
One hand opens, closes down more tightly, the arm extends suddenly
    full length,
jerks once at the end, again, holds: there's a more pronounced elongation
    of the skull—
the infant pudginess, whatever atavism it represented, or reversion, has
    been called back.

Now I sense, although I can't say how, his awareness of me: I can feel
him begin to *think,*
I even know that he's thinking—or thinking in a dream perhaps—of me
here watching him.
Now I'm aware—again, with no notion how, nothing indicates it—that
if there was a dream,
it's gone, and, yes, his eyes abruptly open although his gaze, straight
before him,
seems not to register just yet, the mental operations still independent of
his vision.
I say his name, the way we do it, softly, calling one another from a cove
or cave,
as though something else were there with us, not to be disturbed, to be
crept along beside.
The lids come down again, he yawns, widely, very consciously mani-
festing intentionality.
Great, if rudimentary, pleasure now: a sort of primitive, peculiarly mam-
malian luxury—
to know, to know wonderfully that lying here, warm, protected, eyes
closed, one can,
for a moment anyway, a precious instant, put off the lower specie onsets,
duties, debts.
Sleeker, somehow, slyer, more aggressive now, he is suddenly more
awake, all awake,
already plotting, scheming, fending off: nothing said but there is mild
rebellion, conflict:
I insist, he resists, and then, with abrupt, wriggling grace, he otters down
from sight,
just his brow and crown, his shining rumpled hair, left ineptly showing
from the sheet.
Which I pull back to find him in what he must believe a parody of sleep,
himself asleep:
fetal, rigid, his arms clamped to his sides, eyes screwed shut, mouth
clenched, grinning.

Neglect

An old hill town in northern Pennsylvania, a missed connection for a
    bus, an hour to kill.
For all intents and purposes, the place was uninhabited; the mines had
    closed years before—
anthracite too dear to dig, the companies went west to strip, the miners
    to the cities—
and now, although the four-lane truck route still went through—eigh-
    teen-wheelers pounding past—
that was almost all: a shuttered Buick dealer, a grocery, not even a
    McDonald's,
just the combination ticket office, luncheonette and five-and-dime where
    the buses turned around.
A low gray frame building, it was gloomy and rundown, but charmingly
    old-fashioned:
ancient wooden floors, open shelves, the smell of unwrapped candy,
    cigarettes and band-aid glue.
The only people there, the only people I think that I remember from the
    town at all,
were the silent woman at the register and a youngish teen-aged boy
    standing reading.
The woman smoked and smoked, stared out the streaky window, handed
    me my coffee with indifference.
It was hard to tell how old she was: her hair was dyed and teased, iced
    into a beehive.
The boy was frail, sidelong somehow, afflicted with a devastating Nessus-
    shirt of acne
boiling down his face and neck—pits and pores, scarlet streaks and scars;
    saddening.
We stood together at the magazine rack for a while before I realized
    what he was looking at.
Pornography: two naked men, one grimaces, the other, with a fist inside
    the first one, grins.

I must have flinched: the boy sidled down, blanked his face more and
    I left to take a walk.
It was cold, but not enough to catch or clear your breath: uncertain
    clouds, unemphatic light.
Everything seemed dimmed and colorless, the sense of surfaces dissolv-
    ing, like the Parthenon.
Farther down the main street were a dentist and a chiropractor, both
    with hand-carved signs,
then the Elks' decaying clapboard mansion with a parking space "Re-
    served for the Exalted Ruler,"
and a Russian church, gilt onion domes, a four-horned air-raid siren on
    a pole between them.
Two blocks in, the old slate sidewalks shatter and uplift—gnawed lawns,
    aluminum butane tanks—
then the roads begin to peter out and rise: half-fenced yards with scabs
    of weeks-old snow,
thin, inky, oily leaks of melt insinuating down the gulleys and the cin-
    dered cuts
that rose again into the footings of the filthy, disused slagheaps ringing
    the horizon.
There was nowhere else. At the depot now, the woman and the boy
    were both behind the counter.
He was on a stool, his eyes closed, she stood just in back of him,
    massaging him,
hauling at his shoulders, kneading at the muscles like a boxer's trainer
    between rounds.
I picked up the county paper: it was anti-crime and welfare bums, for
    Reaganomics and defense.
The wire-photo was an actress in her swimming suit, that famously
    expensive bosom, cream.
My bus arrived at last, its heavy, healthy white exhaust pouring in the
    afternoon.
Glancing back, I felt a qualm, concern, an ill heart, almost parental, but
    before I'd hit the step,
the boy'd begun to blur, to look like someone else, the woman had
    already faded absolutely.

All that held now was that violated, looted country, the fraying fringes
        of the town,
those gutted hills, hills by rote, hills by permission, great, naked wastes
        of wrack and spill,
vivid and disconsolate, like genitalia shaved and disinfected for an
        operation.

Still Life

All we do—how old are we? I must be twelve, she a little older; thirteen,
    fourteen—is hold hands
and wander out behind a barn, past a rusty hay rake, a half-collapsed
    old Model T,
then down across a barbed-wire gated pasture—early emerald ryegrass,
    sumac in the dip—
to where a brook, high with run-off from a morning storm, broadened
    and spilled over—
turgid, muddy, viscous, snagged here and there with shattered
    branches—in a bottom meadow.

I don't know then that the place, a mile from anywhere, and day, bril-
    liant, sultry, balmy,
are intensifying everything I feel, but I know now that what made simply
    touching her
almost a consummation was as much the light, the sullen surge of water
    through the grass,
the coils of scent, half hers—the unfamiliar perspiration, talc, something
    else I'll never place—
and half the air's: mown hay somewhere, crushed clover underfoot, the
    brook, the breeze.

I breathe it still, that breeze, and, not knowing how I know for certain
    that it's that,
although it is, I know, exactly that, I drag it in and drive it—rich,
    delicious,
as biting as wet tin—down, my mind casting up flickers to fit it—another
    field, a hollow—
and now her face, even it, frail and fine, comes momentarily to focus,
    and her hand,
intricate and slim, the surprising firmness of her clasp, how judiciously
    it meshes mine.

All we do—how long does it last? an hour or two, not even one whole
      afternoon:
I'll never see her after that, and, strangely (strange even now), not mind,
      as though,
in that afternoon the revelations weren't only of the promises of flesh,
      but of resignation—
all we do is trail along beside the stream until it narrows, find the one-
      log bridge
and cross into the forest on the other side: silent footfalls, hills, a crest,
      a lip.

I don't know then how much someday—today—I'll need it all, how
      much want to hold it,
and, not knowing why, not knowing still how time can tempt us so
      emphatically and yet elude us,
not have it, not the way I would, not the way I want to have *that* day,
      that light,
the motes that would have risen from the stack of straw we leaned on
      for a moment,
the tempered warmth of air which so precisely seemed the coefficient of
      my fearful ardor,

not, after all, even the objective place, those shifting paths I can't really
      follow now
but only can compile from how many other ambles into other woods,
      other stoppings in a glade—
(for a while we were lost, and frightened; night was just beyond the
      hills; we circled back)—
even, too, her gaze, so darkly penetrating, then lifting idly past, is so
      much imagination,
a portion of that figured veil we cast against oblivion, then try, with
      little hope, to tear away.

The Regulars

In the Colonial Luncheonette on Sixth Street they know everything there
      is to know, the shits.
Sam Terminadi will tell you how to gamble yourself at age sixty from
      accountant to bookie,
and Sam Finkel will tell you more than anyone cares to hear how to
      parlay an ulcer into a pension
so you can sit here drinking this shit coffee and eating these overfried
      shit eggs
while you explain that the reasons the people across the street are going
      to go bust
in the toy store they're redoing the old fish market into—the father and
      son plastering,
putting up shelves, scraping the floors; the mother laboring over the
      white paint,
even the daughter coming from school to mop the century of scales and
      splatter from the cellar—
are both simple and complex because Sam T can tell you the answer to
      anything in the world
in one word and Sam F prefaces all his I-told-you-so's with "You don't
      understand, it's complex."
"It's simple," Sam T says, "where around here is anyone going to get
      money for toys?" The end.
Never mind the neighborhood's changing so fast that the new houses
      at the end of the block
are selling for twice what the whole block would have five years ago,
      that's not the point.
Business shits, right? Besides, the family—what's that they're eating?—
      are wrong, right?
Not totally wrong, what are they, Arabs or something? but still, wrong
      enough, that's sure.
"And where do they live?" Sam F asks. "Sure as shit their last dime's
      in the lease and shit sure
they'll end up living in back of the store like gypsies, guaranteed: didn't
      I tell you or not

when the Minskys were still here that they'd bug out first chance they
     got, and did they or no?"
Everyone thought the Minsky brothers would finally get driven out of
     their auto repair shop
by zoning or by having their tools stolen so many times, Once, Frank
     Minsky would growl,
on Yom Kippur, for crying out loud, but no, at the end, they just sold,
     they'd worked fifty years,
And Shit, Frank said, that's fucking enough, we're going to Miami, what
     do you want from me?
But Sam F still holds it against them, to cave in like that, the buggers,
     bastards, shits . . .
What he really means, Sam, Sam, is that everyone misses the Minskys'
     back room, where they'd head,
come dusk, the old boys, and there'd be the bottle of schnapps and the
     tits from *Playboy*
in the grimy half-dark with the good stink of three lifetimes of grease
     and sweat and bitching,
and how good that would be, back then, oh, how far back was then?
     Last year, is that all?
"They got no class: shit, a toy store," Sam T says. What does that mean,
     Sam? What class?
*No class, that's all, simple: six months there and boom, they'll have a
     fire, guaranteed.*
Poor Sam, whether the last fire, at the only butcher store for blocks the
     A&P hadn't swallowed,
was arson for insurance as Sam proved the next day, or whether, the
     way the firemen saw it,
it was just a bum keeping warm in the alley, Sam's decided to take it
     out on the strangers,
glaring at them over there in their store of dreams, their damned pain-
     in-the-ass toy store.
What's the matter with you, are you crazy? is what the father finally
     storms in with one afternoon,
both Sams turning their backs, back to their shit burgers, but old Bernie
     himself is working today,
and *Hey*, Bernie says, *Don't mind them, they're just old shits, sit down,
     I'll buy you a coffee.*

Who the fuck do they think they are? Here have a donut, don't worry,
they'll be all right,
and of course they will be. "In a month you won't get them out of your
hair," says Bernie,
and he's right again, old Bernie, before you know it Sam T has got me
cornered in the street.
"What is it, for Christ's sake, Sam? Let me go." "No, wait up, it's a
computer for kids."
"Sam, please, I'm in a hurry." "No, hold on, just a second, look, it's
simple."

Soon

The whole lower panel of the chain-link fence girdling my old grammar
    school playground
has been stripped from its stanchions and crumpled disdainfully onto
    the shattered pavement.
The upper portion sags forlornly, as though whatever maintenance man
    had to hang it last
was too disheartened doing it again to bother tensioning the guy wires
    to the true.

The building's pale, undistinguished stone is sooty, graffiti cover every
    surface within reach.
Behind their closely woven, galvanized protective mesh, the windows
    are essentially opaque,
but in the kindergarten and first grade I can make out skeletons and
    pumpkins scotch-taped up.
It's Halloween, the lower grades are having their procession and I stop
    awhile to watch.

Except that everyone is black—the kids, the parents looking on, almost
    all the teachers—
my class, when we were out there parading in our costumes, must have
    looked about the same.
Witches, cowboys, clowns, some Supermen and Batmen, a Bo-Peep and
    a vampire.
I don't think we had robots, or not such realistic ones, and they don't
    have an Uncle Sam.

Uncle Sam! *I* was Uncle Sam! I remember! With what ardor I conceived
    my passion to be him.
Uncle Sam. The war was on then, everyone was gaga with it; Uncle Sam
    was everywhere,
recruiting, selling bonds—that poster with its virile, foreshortened finger
    accusing you—

and there, at the local dime store, to my incredulous delight, his outfit
    was.

It must have cost enough to mean something in those days, still half in
    the Depression,
but I dwelled on it . . . The box alone: Uncle Sam was on it in his
    stovepipe, smiling this time,
and there was a tiny window you could see a square of bangles through,
    a ribbon of lapel.
It burned in me, I fretted, nagged: my first instance of our awful fever
    to consume.

When I'd had it half an hour, I hated it—even at that age, I knew when
    I'd been cheated.
Ill-made, shoddy, the gauzy fabric coarsely dyed, with the taste of some-
    thing evil in its odor,
it was waxy with a stiffening that gave it body long enough for you to
    get it on,
then it bagged, and clung, and made you feel the fool you'd been to
    want it in the first place.

The little patriot in his wounded rage of indignation; hold your tongue,
    I told myself.
My itchy cotton-batting beard was pasted on: so much anyway of ed-
    ucation went against my will.
Fold your hands, raise your hands, the Pledge of Allegiance, prayers and
    air-raid drills.
We were taught obsessively to be "Good Citizens," a concept I never
    quite understood.

How the city's changed since then: downtown, businesses have fled,
    whole blocks are waste,
all that's left of what went on between the rioters and Guard tanks in
    the sixties.
Here, even the fieldhouse on the ballpark where they gave us nature
    lectures is in shambles:
the grass is gone, a frowsy gorse has sprouted from the brick- and bottle-
    ridden rubble.

The baskets on their court are still intact at least, although the metal
    nets are torn.
Some men who must be from the neighborhood have got a game going
    out there now.
The children circle shyly, hand in hand, as solemn as a frieze of Greeks,
    while a yard beyond,
the backboards boom, the players sweat and feint and drive, as though
    everything depended on it.

The Gas Station

This is before I'd read Nietzsche. Before Kant or Kierkegaard, even before
    Whitman and Yeats.
I don't think there were three words in my head yet. I knew, perhaps,
    that I should suffer,
I can remember I almost cried for this or for that, nothing special, nothing
    to speak of.
Probably I was mad with grief for the loss of my childhood, but I
    wouldn't have known that.
It's dawn. A gas station. Route twenty-two. I remember exactly: route
    twenty-two curved,
there was a squat, striped concrete divider they'd put in after a plague
    of collisions.
The gas station? Texaco, Esso—I don't know. They were just words
    anyway then, just what their signs said.
I wouldn't have understood the first thing about monopoly or imperialist
    or oppression.
It's dawn. It's so late. Even then, when I was never tired, I'm just holding
    on.
Slumped on my friend's shoulder, I watch the relentless, wordless misery
    of the route twenty-two sky
that seems to be filming my face with a grainy oil I keep trying to rub
    off or in.
Why are we here? Because one of my friends, in the men's room over
    there, has blue balls.
He has to jerk off. I don't know what that means, "blue balls," or why
    he has to do that—
it must be important to have to stop here after this long night, but I
    don't ask.
I'm just trying, I think, to keep my head as empty as I can for as long
    as I can.
One of my other friends is asleep. He's so ugly, his mouth hanging, slack
    and wet.
Another—I'll never see this one again—stares from the window as
    though he were frightened.

Here's what we've done. We were in Times Square, a pimp found us, corralled us, led us somewhere,

down a dark street, another dark street, up dark stairs, dark hall, dark apartment,

where his whore, his girl or his wife or his mother for all I know dragged herself from her sleep,

propped herself on an elbow, gazed into the dark hall, and agreed, for two dollars each, to take care of us.

Take care of us. Some of the words that come through me now seem to stay, to hook in.

My friend in the bathroom is taking so long. The filthy sky must be starting to lighten.

It took me a long time, too, with the woman, I mean. Did I mention that she, the woman, the whore or mother,

was having her time and all she would deign do was to blow us? Did I say that? Deign? Blow?

What a joy, though, the idea was in those days. Blown! What a thing to tell the next day.

She only deigned, though, no more. She was like a machine. When I lift her back to me now,

there's nothing there but that dark, curly head, working, a machine, up and down, and now,

Freud, Marx, Fathers, tell me, what am I, doing this, telling this, on her, on myself,

hammering it down, cementing it, sealing it in, but a machine, too? *Why am I doing this?*

I still haven't read Augustine. I don't understand Chomsky that well. Should I?

My friend at last comes back. Maybe the right words were there all along. *Complicity. Wonder.*

How pure we were then, before Rimbaud, before Blake. *Grace. Love. Take care of us. Please.*

Tar

The first morning of Three Mile Island: those first disquieting, uncertain,
    mystifying hours.
All morning a crew of workmen have been tearing the old decrepit roof
    off our building,
and all morning, trying to distract myself, I've been wandering out to
    watch them
as they hack away the leaden layers of asbestos paper and disassemble
    the disintegrating drains.
After half a night of listening to the news, wondering how to know a
    hundred miles downwind
if and when to make a run for it and where, then a coming bolt awake
    at seven
when the roofers we've been waiting for since winter sent their ladders
    shrieking up our wall,
we still know less than nothing: the utility company continues making
    little of the accident,
the slick federal spokesmen still have their evasions in some semblance
    of order.
Surely we suspect now we're being lied to, but in the meantime, there
    are the roofers,
setting winch-frames, sledging rounds of tar apart, and there I am, on
    the curb across, gawking.

I never realized what brutal work it is, how matter-of-factly and har-
    rowingly dangerous.
The ladders flex and quiver, things skid from the edge, the materials are
    bulky and recalcitrant.
When the rusty, antique nails are levered out, their heads pull off; the
    underroofing crumbles.
Even the battered little furnace, roaring along as patient as a donkey,
    chokes and clogs,
a dense, malignant smoke shoots up, and someone has to fiddle with a
    cock, then hammer it,

before the gush and stench will deintensify, the dark, Dantean broth
      wearily subside.
In its crucible, the stuff looks bland, like licorice, spill it, though, on
      your boots or coveralls,
it sears, and everything is permeated with it, the furnace gunked with
      burst and half-burst bubbles,
the men themselves so completely slashed and mucked they seem almost
      from another realm, like trolls.
When they take their break, they leave their brooms standing at attention
      in the asphalt pails,
work gloves clinging like Br'er Rabbit to the bitten shafts, and they
      slouch along the precipitous lip,
the enormous sky behind them, the heavy noontime air alive with shim-
      mers and mirages.

Sometime in the afternoon I had to go inside: the advent of our vigil
      was upon us.
However much we didn't want to, however little we would do about
      it, we'd understood:
we were going to perish of all this, if not now, then soon, if not soon,
      then someday.
Someday, some final generation, hysterically aswarm beneath an at-
      mosphere as unrelenting as rock,
would rue us all, anathematize our earthly comforts, curse our surfeits
      and submissions.
I think I know, though I might rather not, why my roofers stay so clear
      to me and why the rest,
the terror of that time, the reflexive disbelief and distancing, all we should
      hold on to, dims so.
I remember the president in his absurd protective booties, looking ab-
      solutely unafraid, the fool.
I remember a woman on the front page glaring across the misty Sus-
      quehanna at those looming stacks.
But, more vividly, the men, silvered with glitter from the shingles, cling-
      ing like starlings beneath the eaves.

Even the leftover carats of tar in the gutter, so black they seemed to
suck the light out of the air.
By nightfall kids had come across them: every sidewalk on the block
was scribbled with obscenities and hearts.

One of the Muses

I

I will not grace you with a name . . . Even "you," however modest the
     convention: not here.
No need here for that much presence. Let "you" be "she," and let the
     choice, incidentally,
be dictated not by bitterness or fear—a discretion, simply, the most
     inoffensive decorum.

This was, after all, if it needs another reason, long ago, and not just in
     monthly, yearly time,
not only in that house of memory events, the shadowed, off-sized rooms
     of which
it amuses us to flip the doors of like a deck of cards, but also in the
     much more malleable,

mazy, convoluted matter of the psyche itself, especially the wounded
     psyche,
especially the psyche stricken once with furrows of potential which are
     afterwards untenanted:
voids, underminings, to be buttressed with the webbiest filaments of day-
     to-dayness.

2

Long ago, in another place, it seems sometimes in another realm of being
    altogether,
one of those dimensions we're told intersects our own, rests there side
    by side with ours,
liable to be punched across into by charity or prayer, other skullings at
    the muscle.

How much of her essential being can or should be carried over into now
    isn't clear to me.
That past which holds her, yellowed with allusiveness, is also charged
    with unreality:
a tiny theater in whose dim light one senses fearfully the contaminating
    powers of illusion.

Here, in a relatively stable present, no cries across the gorge, no veils
    atremble,
it sometimes seems as though she may have been a fiction utterly, a
    symbol or a system of them.
In any case, what good conceivably could come at this late date of
    recapitulating my afflictions?

3

Apparently, it would have to do with what that ancient desperation
    means to me today.
We recollect, call back, surely not to suffer; is there something then for
    me, today,
something lurking, potent with another loss, this might be meant to alter
    or avert?

No, emphatically: let it be that simple. And not any sort of longing
    backwards, either:
no desire to redeem defeats, no humiliations to atone for, no expiations
    or maledictions.

Why bother then? Why inflict it on myself again, that awful time, those
    vacillations and frustrations?

It's to be accounted for, that's all. Something happened, the time has
    come to find its place.
Let it just be that: not come to terms with, not salvage something from,
    not save.
There was this, it's to be accounted for: "she," for that, will certainly
    suffice.

4

She had come to me . . . *She* to *me* . . . I know that, I knew it then,
    however much, at the end,
trying so to hang on to it, to keep something of what by then was
    nothing, I came to doubt,
to call the memory into question, that futile irreducible of what had
    happened and stopped happening.

She, to me, and with intensity, directness, aggression even, an aggression
    that may have been,
I think, the greater part of my involvement to begin with: in the sweep
    of her insistence,
it was as though she'd simply shouldered past some debilitating shyness
    on my part,

some misgiving, some lack of faith I'd never dared acknowledge in myself
    but which, now,
I suddenly understood had been a part of my most basic being: a tearing
    shoal of self,
which, brought to light now, harrowingly recognized, had flowed away
    beneath me.

5

Later, when everything had turned, fallen, but when we still found ways,
    despite it all,

through our impediments—my grief, her ever-stricter panels of reserve—
    that first consummation,
her power, the surprising counter-power I answered with, came to seem
    a myth, a primal ceremony.

Later, and not much later because the start and end were, although I
    couldn't bear to think it,
nearly one, it became almost a ritual, not even ritual, a repetition, and
    I had to recognize,
at last, how few times that first real, unqualified soaring had actually
    been enacted.

Maybe several times, maybe only once: once and once—that would have
    been enough,
enough to keep me there, to keep me trying to recuperate it, so long
    after I'd begun to feel,
and to acknowledge to myself, her searing hesitations, falterings, awk-
    wardnesses.

6

Her withholdings were so indefinite at first, it wasn't hard to fend them
    off, deny them.
The gasp that seemed—but did it really?—to extend a beat into a sigh,
    and then the sigh,
did it go on an extra instant to become a heave of tedium, impatience,
    resignation?

. . . Then the silences: I could have, if I'd wanted to, dared to, been
    certain of the silences.
They were in time, had duration, could be measured: how I must have
    wanted not to know.
I didn't even name them that at first, "silence," no: lapses, inattentions,
    respites.

It feels as though I'd begun to try to cope with them before I'd actually
    remarked them.

They weren't silences until they'd flared and fused, until her silences
    became her silence,
until we seemed, to my chagrin, my anguish, horror, to be wholly in
    and of them.

7

Her silence: how begin to speak of it? I think sometimes I must have
    simply gaped.
There were harmonies in it, progressions, colors, resolutions: it was a
    symphony, a tone poem.
I seemed to live in it, it was always with me, a matrix, background
    sound: surf, wind.

Sometimes, when I'd try to speak myself, I'd find it had insinuated into
    my voice:
it would haul at me; I'd go hoarse, metallic, hollow, nothing that I said
    entailed.
More and more her presence seemed preceded by it: a quiet on the stair,
    hushed hall.

I'd know before I heard her step that she was with me, and when she'd
    go, that other,
simpler silence, after all the rest, was like a coda, magnificent, absorbing,
one last note reverberating on and on, subdividing through its physics
    toward eternity.

8

At the same time, though, it was never, never quite, defined as being
    final.
She always, I have no idea how, left her clef of reticence ajar: a lace, a
    latticework.
I thought—I think that I was meant to think—it was provisional, a
    stopping place.

And, to exacerbate things, it became her: with it, and within it, she
    seemed to promise more.

The sheer *focus* it demanded; such shadings were implied in how she
   turned in it;
the subtleties I hadn't been allowed, the complexities not fathomed: she
   was being re-enhanced by it.

What was inaccessible in her, what not, what—even as I'd hold her,
   even as we'd touch—
was being drawn away, marked off, forbidden: such resonance between
   potential and achieved.
The vibrations, though, as subtle as they were, crystalline, were tearing
   me apart.

9

Sometimes, it would seem as though, still with me, she had already left
   me.
Sometimes, later, when she really had left, left again, I would seem to
   ache,
not with the shocks or after-shocks of passion, but with simply holding
   her, holding on.

Sometimes, so flayed, I would think that I was ready to accept defeat,
   ready to concede.
I may have even wished for hints of concrete evidence from her that she
   wanted us to stop.
She could, I thought, with the gentlest move, have disengaged: I was
   ready for it . . .

No, not so, I wasn't. Wasn't what was wrong so slight, so patently
   inconsequential to the rest?
If I let her go like that, I thought, how would I ever know that what
   had brought us down
wasn't merely my own dereliction or impatience? No, there had to be
   a way to solve this.

10

I kept thinking: there is something which, if said in precisely the right
   words to her . . .

I kept thinking, there's an explanation I can offer, an analysis, maybe just a way of saying,
a rhythm or a rhetoric, to fuse the strands of her ambivalence and draw her back.

I kept thinking—she may have kept me thinking—there's something I haven't understood about her,
something I've misconceived or misconstrued, something I've missed the message of and offended . . .
I'd set theories up from that, programs, and, with notes along the way toward future tries,

I'd elaborate the phrases, paragraphs, the volumes of my explication: I'd rehearse them,
offer them, and have her, out of hand, hardly noticing, reject, discard, disregard them,
until I learned myself—it didn't take me long—out of hand, hardly noticing, to discard them.

II

Sometimes, though, I'd imagine that something—yes—I'd said would reach her.
Her presence, suddenly, would seem to soften, there would be a flood of ease, a decontraction.
She'd be with me, silent still, but *there,* and I would realize how far she'd drifted.

I wouldn't know then, having her, or thinking that I did, whether to be miserable or pleased.
I'd go on, even so, to try to seal it, build on it, extend, certify it somehow,
and then, suddenly again, I'd sense that she'd be gone again, or, possibly, much worse,

had never been there, or not the way I'd thought it for that thankful instant.
I'd misinterpreted, misread, I'd have to start my search again, my trial, travail.

Where did I ever find the energy for it? Just to think about it now exhausts
    me.

12

Wherever I did find the strength, half of it I dedicated to absolving and
    forgiving her.
Somehow I came to think, and never stopped believing, I was inflicting
    all my anguish on myself.
She was blameless, wasn't she? Her passivity precluded else: the issue
    had to be with me.

I tried to reconceive myself, to situate myself in the syntax of our crippled
    sentence.
I parsed myself, searching out a different flow for the tangle of amputated
    phrases I was by then.
Nothing, though, would sound, would scan, no matter how I carved,
    dissected, chopped.

I couldn't find the form, the meter, rhythm, or, by now, the barest context
    for myself.
I became a modifier: my only function was to alter the conditions of
    this fevered predication.
I became a word one thinks about too closely: clumps of curves and
    serifs, the arbitrary symbol of itself.

13

I became, I became . . . Finally, I think I must have simply ceased even
    that, becoming.
I was an image now, petrified, unmediated, with no particular associ-
    ation, no connotation,
certainly no meaning, certainly no hope of ever being anything that bore
    a meaning.

It was as though my identity had been subsumed in some enormous
    generalization,

one so far beyond my comprehension that all I could know was that I
    was incidental to it,
that with me or without me it would grind along the complex epicycles
    of its orbit.

It was as though the system I'd been living in had somehow suddenly
    evolved beyond me.
I had gills to breathe a stratosphere, and my hopeless project was to
    generate new organs,
new lobes to try to comprehend this emotional ecology, and my ex-
    tinction in it.

14

The hours, the labor: how I wracked my mind, how my mind revenged
    itself on me.
I was wild, helpless, incapable of anything at all by now but watching
    as I tore myself.
I huddled there at the center of myself and tried to know by some reflexive
    act of faith

that I'd survive all this, this thing, my self, that mauled and savaged me.
I'd behold it all, so much frenzy, so many groans and bellows; even
    now, watching now,
I seem to sink more deeply into some protective foliage: I tremble in
    here, quake,

and then I dart—even now, still, my eyes, despite me, dart: walls, floor,
    sky—
I dart across that field of fear, away, away from there, from here, from
    anywhere.
I was frightened sometimes that I might go mad. And then I did just
    that—go mad.

15

It was like another mind, my madness, my blessèd, holy madness: no,
    it *was* another mind.

It arrives, my other mind, on another night when I'm without her, hoping, or past hope.
My new mind comes upon me with a hush, a fluttering, a silvery ado, and it has a volume,

granular and sensitive, which exactly fits the volume of the mind I already have.
Its desire seems to be to displace that other mind, and something in me—how say what?
how explain the alacrity of such a radical concurrence?—decides to let it,

and the split second of the decision and the onset of the workings of that mind are instantaneous.
In one single throb of intuition I understood what the function of my mind was,
because, in and of it now, convinced, absorbed, I was already working out its implications.

16

I knew already that my other mind—I hardly could recall it—had had a flaw and from that flaw
had been elaborated a delusion, and that delusion in its turn was at the base of all my suffering,
all the agonies I'd been inflicting, so unnecessarily, I understood, upon myself.

I had thought, I realized, that reality of experience, data and events, were to be received,
that perception, sensory, experiential accumulation, was essentially passive,
that it accepted what was offered and moved within that given, the palpable or purely mental,

partaking of it as it could, jiggling the tenuous impressions here or there a bit,

a sentence added, or a chapter, but nothing more than that: we were
      almost victims,
or if not victims quite, not effective agents surely, not of anything that
      mattered.

17

What my new mind made me understand, though the facts had been
      there all the while before my eyes,
was that reality, as I'd known it, as I knew it now, was being generated,
      every second,
out of me and by me: it was me, myself, and no one else, who spun it
      out this way.

It was my own will, unconscious until now but now with purpose and
      intent, which made the world.
Not made-up, which implies imagination or idea, but made, actually
      created, everything,
in a flow, a logic, a succession of events, I could trace now with my very
      blood.

Even time: looking back at the wash of time on earth, it, too, was a
      function of this moment.
Then cosmic time was flowing, too, from the truth I was living now,
      not for myself now,
for my salvation or survival, but for the infinitely vulnerable fact of
      existence itself.

18

Does it matter very much what the rest was, the odd conclusions I kept
      coming to?
What really seems important was that even as it happened, even as I let
      it happen,
even as I held it in a sort of mental gale—it wasn't necessary then to
      work it out like this,

all of it was there at once, in a single block, entire, a kind of geometric
    bliss—
I understood that it was all hallucination and delusion, that these insights
    or illuminations
were wretched figments of emotion all, but I didn't care, I let them take
    me further,

past proposition, syllogism, sense: I was just a premise mechanism now,
    an epistemology machine;
I let my field of vision widen—everything was mine now, coal and comet,
    root and moon,
all found their footing, fulfilled at last, in my felicity, and then, rendingly,
    it ended.

19

Why it stopped was as much a mystery to me as why it should have
    happened in the first place,
but when it did, something else took its place, a sort of vision, or a
    partial vision,
or at least a knowledge, as instantly accessible and urgent as the other,
    and, I'd find, as fleeting.

Somehow, I knew, I'd touched into the very ground of self, its axioms
    and assumptions,
and what was there wasn't what I'd thought—I hadn't *known* what I'd
    thought but knew it now—
not violence, not conflagration, sexual turbulence, a philosophic or emo-
    tive storm,

but a sort of spiritual erasure, a nothingness of motive and intention,
    and I understood, too,
in another bolt, that all that keeps us from that void, paradoxically
    perhaps, is trust . . .
Trust in what? Too late: that perception, too, was gone; I had to watch
    another revelation end.

20

But not badly, even so . . . I came back, to myself, feeling not contrite,
 not embarrassed,
certainly not frightened . . . awkward, maybe, toward myself, shy,
 abashed: I couldn't, as it were,
meet the gaze of this stranger I was in a body with, but I couldn't, either,
 take my eyes away.

Something had altered, *I* had: there was something unfamiliar, incon-
 gruous about me.
I couldn't specify exactly, not at first, what I felt; it wasn't, though,
 unpleasant.
I probed myself as though I'd had an accident; nothing broken, I was
 all right, more:

a sense of lightness, somehow, a change in my specific gravity, a relief,
 unburdening,
and then I knew, with no fuss or flourish, what it was: she, she wasn't
 with me now,
she was gone from me, from either of my minds, all my minds, my
 selves—she simply wasn't there.

21

I could say it feels as though I'm taking breaths: she is gone and gone,
 he, shriven of her,
leaps into his life, but as I went about the work of understanding what
 had happened to me,
who I was now, it was clear at once that my having torn myself from
 her was unimportant.

She was gone, why she'd been there to begin with, what I'd seen in her,
 thought she'd meant,
why I'd let that suffering come to me, became immediately the most
 theoretical of questions.
That I'd have to be without her now meant only that: without her, not
 forlorn, bereft.

I even tested cases: if she went on to someone else, touched someone
        else, would I envy them,
her touch, her fire? Not even that: her essence for me was her being
        with me for that time,
with someone else, she, too, was other than herself: a wraith, a formula
        or intellection.

22

I felt no regret—indifference, rather, a flare of disbelief, then an unex-
        pected moment of concern.
Had she suffered, too? Had she even sensed, in her empyrean distance,
        that this,
any of it, was going on at all? I didn't answer then, if I had to now, I'd
        have to doubt it.

I think that, after those first moments, she was gone already from me:
        perhaps, though,
it's not my task to try to answer, perhaps all I really have the right to
        do is ask
what the person I am now might have to do with her, wraith or not,
        memory of a memory or not?

Was I enhanced by her? Diminished by her? All that's really sure is that
        if I was changed,
it wasn't the embrace, the touch, that would have done it, but what
        came after, her withdrawal,
her painful non-responses, her absence and the ever more incorporeal
        innuendos in that absence.

23

And my "madness," that business of the other mind, that "trust": have
        I taken anything from that?
Perhaps. I think I'd always realized the possibility was there for us to
        do that to ourselves,
undo ourselves that way, not in suicide, but in something much more
        dire, complete, denying.

I think that I'd suspected, too, that with the means to do it, I would
  someday have to do it.
And now, what I'd been afraid I'd do, I'd done: that she'd had to drive
  me to it didn't matter,
although probably without her, without what she'd inflicted on me, I'd
  have never come to it.

Perhaps, with her abrasive offerings and takings-back, I'd been ground
  down like a lens:
I'd had, to my horror, really to look within myself, into the greater sea
  of chaos there,
and I'd survived it, shaken but intact, with auras, even, of a kind of
  gratitude.

24

What I'm left with after all this time is still the certainty that something
  was attained,
though all that remain now are flickers, more and more occasional, more
  disjointed—
pale remnants of the harsh collaborations those intermediary silences
  symbolized so well.

And this . . . I mean *this*, these lines, constructions, études: these small
  histories,
where did this come from? As I said, there was no desire to go over all
  of it again,
but, after all, whatever ambivalence I felt about it, it demanded care,
  even labor.

The need for doing it never quite defined itself: it, like her, came uncalled
  for.
A tone took me, an impulse toward a structure: I found it interesting,
  a question of aesthetics.
If that were so, might there be another way, another mode in which to
  come to it?

The proposition now could be that this *is* she, this, itself, wholly
    "she."
Not an artifact, not a net in which some wingèd thing protests or pines,
    but her,
completely fused now, inspiration, outcome: she would be, now, what
    she herself effected,

the tones themselves, the systems she wrought from the conflicting musics
    of my conscience.
This time it would be that all she meant to me were these attempts,
    these uncertain colorations,
that took so long to get here, from so far, and from which she would
    be departing now at last,

not into another hesitation, pause, another looking back reluctantly on
    either of our parts—
no turnings, no farewells—but a final sundering, a seeing-off, a last,
    definitely indicated,
precisely scored—no rests, diminuendos, decrescendos—silencing, and
    silence.

Index of Titles

Index of First Lines

I will not grace you with a name . . . Even "you," however modest the convention:
    not here, 220
my face ends inside you, 95
My friend Dave knew a famous writer who used to have screwdrivers for breakfast,
    161
My soul is out back eating your soul, 32
Never on one single pore Eternity, 29
not bad mouth, 103
now she was waiting, 156
our poor angel how sick, 76
probably death fits all right in the world, 104
put mommy on the front steps, 74
Remember me? I was the one, 17
right off we started inflicting history, 85
somebody keeps track of how many times, 73
Some people, 46
something to dip myself into, 92
Spring: the first morning when that one true block of sweet, laminar, complex scent
    arrives, 175
suppose I move a factory, 14
the bottom of the universe and, 112
The first morning of Three Mile Island: those first disquieting, uncertain, mystifying
    hours, 217
the goddamned animals might know more than we do about some things, 97
the grandmas are all coming down like f-101's like gulls, 77
The last party before I left was in an old, run-down apartment house, The Greystone
    Arms, 184
the little children have been fighting, 63
the lonely people are marching, 64
The man who owns sleep, 12
The men working on the building going up here have got these great, 135
The morning is so gray that the grass is gray and the side of the white horse grazing,
    190
the nations have used up their desire, 67
the not want, 113
the only way it makes sense, 86
the pillows are going insane, 80
the president of my country his face flushed, 101
there are people whose sex, 5
There hasn't been any rain, 21